# TO SAVE THE ANIMALS

Library of Congress Control Number: 2015916144

Photo credits:

Front cover (photo of painting): Paul Mailloux

Back cover (photo): Marcel Rodriguez

Painting for front cover by Kate Jewel

Cover design by Kate Jewel

Printed on recycled paper

*for animals and animal lovers*

# Thank You

Thanks to Sharon, Roxy, Nina and Krista for our conversations while I was researching and writing *To Save the Animals,* and to Karen, Christey, Molly and Rob at the Springdale library for their help. Thanks to the scientists whose books, documentaries and articles taught me the science included in my book, to conservationists and all the wonderful people who work to save animals, and to the wildlife in Zion, that inspire me and bring me happiness every day.

# Table of Contents

# PRELUDE

## *Zion*

*I find sanctuary and solace*
*at the river's edge,*
*with hummingbirds and herons,*
*deer and damselflies,*
*wild turkeys and water striders*
*and turquoise-tailed lizards*
*scooting this way and that—*
*my friends,*
*my family.*

November 14, 2006, while mountain jogging, my older dog, Niki, and I were assaulted by three dogs. One dog punctured Niki's neck, then the other two joined in to tear the flesh off her belly. As I bent down to save Niki, the dog who initiated the attack grasped my face and tore at my left eye and nose. My brain ceased to function normally. My short-term memory disappeared. I was unable process information—my brain felt like a dark, thick, mucous sponge. Exhaustion never left me, exercise was extraordinarily difficult. My hearing became distorted; sounds were magnified and felt trapped in my head. My sense of smell nearly completely disappeared. As the dogs attacked me, and for a long time afterwards, I felt I could

1

choose to die. My consciousness went to a barren slope where it seemed easy to slide into death, but I wished to stay alive to write a book to help animals. It has taken years of monumental effort to move past the injuries. Over the years, my brain found new ways to remember and to process information. Gradually, through meditation and an organic vegan diet, the post-traumatic stress healed, and I grew strong enough to exercise.

About one-and-a-half years after the attack, I awoke in the night to a melody streaming through my mind like liquid lightning. Thereafter composing began to heal my brain in miraculous ways. Four-and-a-half years ago I moved near Zion National Park. Since moving here, I've studied many sciences. While pursuing a doctorate in music, I devoted months to learning the *Goldberg Variations* by Bach. The mental discipline and persistence acquired during that journey helped me in researching then writing this book.

*To Save the Animals* looks at misinformation and mistaken assumptions that have led to human-caused climate change, mass extinction, deforestation, ocean acidification and deoxygenation, and cruelty to non-human animals. Many people have embraced these notions in the way we once felt certain that the Earth was flat and at the center of the universe. The science in *To Save the Animals* describes the phenomenal beauty and complexity of life. It's thrilling, even if one only understands a little, and, after the DNA section, the science is straightforward.

I start at the beginning of the universe and the formation of the elements, then describe the eukaryote cell, DNA and proteins, which we share with all other animals. After this, the book explores animal intelligence, empathy, digestive physiology and anatomy, to better understand that *Homo sapiens* is a primarily vegetarian species. Linking science to morality, I describe ways to eat and live in order to save life on Earth.

## THE UNIVERSE, STARS, SUN AND THE EARTH

Decades ago I often camped along the Chama River in the northern New Mexico color country past Abiquiu. A million stars fill the sky on moonless nights. The stillness and the sense of the immensity of time and space are glorious to experience. Thus far scientists have discovered life nowhere else in the universe. Earth is a paradise that we are destroying with our diet and lifestyle choices and human population growth. Never has it been more important to see clearly, act wisely, cherish life.

3

Scientists theorize that the universe began with an explosion (the Big Bang) almost 13.8 billion years ago. It is believed that before the Big Bang billions of galaxies all together possibly occupied a space smaller than an electron. There was astonishing activity during first second after the Big Bang. The temperature, 1,000 trillion trillion degrees Celsius, began to drop. The universe may have become incomprehensibly larger (expanding perhaps $10^{78}$ times) in an unimaginably short time (less than $10^{-32}$ seconds). Subatomic particles formed then acquired mass. Protons and neutrons, then nuclei formed during the first minutes. 380,000 to 400,000 years later there were hydrogen, helium and other atoms; the universe is comprised of approximately 75% hydrogen and 25% helium. Light began to shine, and around 100 million years later the first stars formed.

The universe may be infinite. Today the observable universe is 91 billion light years across; a light year is 9.46 x $10^{12}$ km/5.88 trillion mi. There are more than 100 billion galaxies in the observable universe, and each galaxy has from 10 million to a trillion stars. Our galaxy, the Milky Way, with 200-400 billion stars, is around 100,000 light years in diameter and about 1,000 light years thick.

Stars burn hydrogen. When the hydrogen is consumed, the star's core collapses, causing the temperature to rise.

When the temperature reaches 100,000,000°C, the star becomes a red giant that burns helium. As the core heats to 100 million degrees Kelvin and more, carbon-12, present in all life, forms, and carbon and hydrogen nuclei fuse to create oxygen. The biggest, hottest stars form the heavier elements, including sodium, magnesium and iron. When the helium is used up, the star explodes, and oxygen, carbon, hydrogen and other elements form clouds of gas and dust called nebulae. Over time clumps of gas collapse to create new stars.

Our Sun formed 4.75 billion years ago. Later, a disc of ice, dust and gas encircling the Sun formed rings from gravitational attraction. Rings with the most rocks eventually formed the planets of our solar system. The Earth formed 4.56 billion years ago.

The oceans formed over 4 billion years ago, from condensation in the atmosphere and water brought from space by comets. A water molecule consists of two hydrogen atoms and one oxygen atom. There is a slight imbalance, with one side of the molecule more positive, the other side more negative, making water an excellent solvent. 3.8 billion years ago, when the early sea had cooled enough for biochemical reactions to take place, hydrogen, carbon, nitrogen and oxygen formed amino acids and probably ribonucleic acid (RNA)—essential components of life.

## THE ELEMENTS

Hydrogen (H), carbon (C), nitrogen (N) and oxygen (O) are the four most common elements in living organisms. Hydrogen, with one proton and one electron, is the lightest of the 112 named elements, and it is the most common element in the universe. Hydrogen and oxygen form water ($H_2O$), which covers 70% of the Earth's surface.

Carbon, with six protons, has different isotopes, carbon-12 being the most common. Carbon-14 is a naturally occurring radioactive isotope used to date fossils (an isotope is each of two or more forms of an element containing identical numbers of protons but different numbers of neutrons). As it decays, the ratio between carbon-12 and carbon-14 changes; the amount of carbon-14 present can determine the age of a fossil up to 40,000 years old.

Diamonds, graphite, charcoal, soot and coal are all forms of carbon. Graphite is one of the softest substances, while diamonds are the hardest naturally occurring matter. Carbon atoms easily link together; with hydrogen, nitrogen, oxygen and other elements (phosphorus, sulfur, etc.), they form chains and rings that are the physical basis of every living organism. There is a nearly infinite variety of carbon compounds.

One carbon atom and two oxygen atoms form carbon dioxide ($CO_2$). Plants use sunlight to synthesize foods from carbon dioxide and water, producing oxygen as a byproduct. During digestion, animals convert carbohydrates to glucose. Glucose and oxygen combine in mitochondria to produce the energy currency adenosine triphosphate (ATP), with carbon dioxide as a byproduct. Atmospheric carbon dioxide, like all molecules comprised of three or more atoms, absorbs infrared radiation the Earth emits to cool itself, then re-emits it in all directions, including back to Earth. The more fossil fuels we burn, the more atmospheric carbon dioxide there is.

Fusion processes from carbon and hydrogen in supernovae first created nitrogen, an element with the atomic number 7. The Earth's atmosphere consists of about 78% nitrogen. Amino acids, the building blocks for proteins, and nucleic acids are nitrogen-based, but atmospheric nitrogen must be reduced, or 'fixed', to be usable. Lightning causes nitrogen fixation, usually reaching the ground as soil nitrate. Certain kinds of bacteria in the soil and roots of some plant species fix the soil nitrate into an ammonium ion that is converted by plants into nitrogen oxides and amino acids to form proteins and other molecules. Animals obtain nitrogen-based amino acids either by consuming plants or through animal protein consumption—all animals are dependent upon plants, directly or indirectly. Because we are a primarily vegetarian species (see the *Homo sapiens* section), we take an unnecessary, circuitous route when we consume animal protein, one that is causing immeasurable tragedy in the natural world.

Nitrogen combines with three hydrogen atoms to form ammonia ($NH_3$). Synthetic ammonia fertilizers are used in production of one third of the world's food plants to increase yields. During rains and floods, the fertilizer washes into rivers, lakes, the ocean. Nitrogen-driven bacterial and plant growth use up the water's oxygen, leading to dead zones— fish, birds, marine life die. In this context, it is important to understand that an animal-based diet requires many times more plants than does a plant-based diet, as the animals we eat must feed, too. There is more about the harm caused by synthetic fertilizers in the chapter on plants and insects.

Oxygen (atomic number 8) forms around 20% of the Earth's atmosphere; it makes up approximately half of the weight of the Earth's crust and 86% of the weight of the oceans. Oxygen reacts easily with most organic compounds, driving life processes. Until cyanobacteria produced enough oxygen during photosynthesis to fill the sea and air, there could be no oxygen-dependent life. Trees give us oxygen while using and storing carbon dioxide, yet we are rapidly deforesting the Earth.

## FIRST LIFE ON EARTH

Fossil evidence of life dates back perhaps 3.5 billion years. The earliest life, eubacteria and archaebacteria, were prokaryotes, microscopic single-celled organisms without a distinct nucleus or other specialized organelles. There are millions of species in each of these domains. Some species thrive in hot springs, salt flats and other extremely alkaline or acidic environments. Anaerobic bacteria die in the presence of oxygen, producing energy in different ways than photosynthesis; they live in the darkness of hydrothermal vents in the ocean and in our intestines, where they help to digest fiber.

Cyanobacteria are eubacteria that photosynthesized in the early sea. At first oxygen reacted with iron to form rust. Later, 2.5 to 1.85 billion years ago, oxygen began to accumulate in the ocean and in the Earth's atmosphere, turning the skies blue and the sea the beautiful colors it is today. Oxygen-dependent life became possible.

## THE EUKARYOTIC CELL, PROTEINS AND DNA

Around two billion years ago eukaryotic cells, found in all life except eubacteria and archaebacteria, came to exist. A eukaryotic cell has a nucleus containing chromatin (consisting of protein, RNA and DNA), encircled by a nuclear membrane. Outside the nucleus is cytoplasm, a watery or jellylike substance. The cytoplasm is bound by the cell's outer membrane, which controls what may enter or leave the cell. The cell has a cytoskeleton made up of protein filaments. There are numerous membranes within the cytoplasm, such as the endoplasmic reticula, that transport proteins and other organelles. Ribosomes attached to the rough endoplasmic reticula help to synthesize proteins. Great numbers of mitochondria, present in most cells, produce adenosine triphosphate (ATP), the energy transfer molecule; breakage of one phosphate linkage of ATP provides energy for cellular activities. Mitochondria are thought to have been prokaryotes that adapted to living in eukaryotic cells. The cytoplasm also contains thousands of different proteins.

The eukaryotic cell is miraculous and phenomenally complex. [This section includes science that may be challenging for some readers. I have included it because it makes clear how interconnected we are to all other animals, an understanding that can help people to move past species arrogance, which is key to saving life on Earth. If one only takes in how awesome and complex and beautiful cells are, that's enough. After this section, the science is straightforward.] During mitosis, a cell divides into two identical daughter cells with DNA identical to that of the parent cell. The fertilized egg cell develops into a living organism, sometimes with billions or trillions of cells. Cells differentiate into specialized cells such as skin cells, neurons, or blood cells; there are more than 200 different kinds of cells in the human body. Cells group together to form sheets and tissues. The eukaryotic cell made possible the evolution of multi-cellular animals with tissues, organs and systems such as the nervous system, digestive system, respiratory system, cardiovascular system, etc.

Proteins and DNA perform crucial activities in the eukaryotic cell. Understanding protein is a key step to saving life on Earth—misinformation about it has helped to bring about climate change and mass extinction. Proteins, present in every cell, function as structural units, enzymes, hormones and antibodies. A protein molecule consists of a string of 30-10,000 amino acids, averaging 50-2,000. Tremendous numbers of proteins are at work in animals; there are more than 50,000 different proteins in human cells. Thousands of protein molecules, including both maintenance and specialized proteins, are present in a cell. The order and number of amino acids determine a given protein's shape and functions. There are twenty different amino acids in human proteins; nine of them, called essential amino acids, must be obtained by consuming plants or animal-based foods. 10% or less of our protein needs to be replaced daily.

There are around 10,000 various proteins in cell outer membranes. Protein carriers and channels transport molecules to and from the cell, changing shape as necessary. The cytoskeleton consists of protein microfilaments and microtubules. Protein microtubules transport organelles within the cell.

Collagen is the main structural protein in animal connective tissue; fibrils of collagen are twisted into fibers. Ligaments are bands of connective tissue that connect bones or cartilage and hold joints together. Tendons are cords of connective tissue linking skeletal muscles to bones, transmitting the pull caused by muscle contraction. Collagen fibers surrounding bone cells provide tensile strength. Keratin, another structural protein, is found in hair, nails, feathers, beaks, scales, hoofs, claws and horns.

Some hormones are proteins, for example insulin, that regulates blood glucose levels. Blood serum contains the protein albumin and diverse protein antibodies and globulins. Hemoglobin is a red protein that transports oxygen in the blood.

Actin and myosin are motor proteins that form the contractile filaments of muscle cells. Filaments of each are arranged in alternating parallel bundles in muscle cells; they slide past each other in muscle contraction. Motor proteins in cilia on many cell surfaces either cause currents in the surrounding fluid or provide propulsion in some protists. Cilia keep our lungs clean, for instance. Motor proteins in the sperm tail propel the sperm to the ovum in the fallopian tube.

A sodium pump comprised of proteins pumps sodium out of cells and potassium into cells, preventing the cells from bursting with water. A protein machine in mitochondria adds a phosphate group to adenosine diphosphate (ADP), changing it into ATP; when a phosphate link breaks, ATP becomes ADP. Every two minutes a billion ATP molecules are used and replaced. Mitochondria have a double membrane; the inner layer folds inward, forming layers. As glucose and oxygen react, electrons move along these membranes, eventually combining with oxygen to form water. Protons (hydrogen ions) move across the membranes then back, traveling down an electro-chemical gradient through a protein machine that produces ATP. The breakdown of a molecule of glucose provides around 30 molecules of ATP (*How We Live*, 37-8).

Enzymes are catalysts—long thin protein strands that speed up a chemical reaction, sometimes a million times! An enzyme may act on 1,000 molecules every second. An enzyme can fold in various ways. It may create a cavity where a molecule fits in to break apart, or it may bring two molecules together to build a larger molecule. Digestive enzymes break down food into units small enough to pass through the intestinal walls into the bloodstream, and they assemble proteins from amino acids. Amylase, found in human saliva and pancreatic fluid, converts starch and glycogen into simple sugars; maltase splits maltose into glucose. Pepsin breaks down proteins into polypeptides, protease breaks down proteins and peptides into amino acids, and peptidase breaks down peptides into amino acids, to be reassembled into proteins the body needs. Lipase is a pancreatic enzyme that breaks down fats into fatty acids and glycerol or other alcohols.

To synthesize a protein, proteins called transcription factors bind to control regions of the gene of the protein to be manufactured. A protein machine in the nucleus transfers the genetic code from deoxyribonucleic acid (DNA) to messenger ribonucleic acid (mRNA). During this transcription phase, the protein machine pulls apart the section of DNA that codes for the selected protein. Noncoding sections of the mRNA, called introns, are removed. The coding parts, called exons, occur in a specific order determined by the protein being synthesized.

The mRNA strand leaves the nucleus, going to a ribosome in the cytoplasm where proteins are synthesized; ribosomes are comprised of protein and RNA. The mRNA is organized in groups of three nucleotides called codons; the order of bases in a codon provides the code for a specific amino acid. In the translation phase, transfer ribonucleic acid (tRNA), also organized in triplet codons, binds to the appropriate amino acid, fits onto the mRNA codon with matching base pairs to deliver it, then breaks off to bind to another amino acid. A chain of amino acids is built into a protein this way; the process takes from 20 seconds to 4 minutes. The length and order of the amino acid string determines how the protein will fold and therefore its function(s).

Proteins and DNA interact in awe-inspiring ways in the cells of plants and animals. Science awakens a sense of wonder as it reveals the unity between ourselves and other species. Science is an ally, not adversary. The more we understand and treasure life, the less inclined we will be to destroy it.

In 1944 DNA was discovered to be the carrier of genetic information. Every gene provides the code to construct a protein or polypeptide. The human genome has around 22,000 genes, contained in 46 chromosomes; stretched out their length would total 2m/6.5'. There are 22 equivalent pairs of chromosomes, one of each pair from the mother, the other from the father, and two sex chromosomes; female sex chromosomes are signified as XX and male sex chromosomes as XY.

A DNA molecule consists of two intertwined spiral strands connected by interlinking base pairs; the helix completes a twist every 10.4 pairs. DNA is like a spiral staircase, with each base pair a ladder rung. The double helix design allows the chromosomes to fit into the nucleus of a microscopic cell, and it makes self-replication possible.

There are 3.2 billion base pairs in the human genome. Each gene has from hundreds to millions of base pairs, occurring in a specific sequence.

Like amino acids, the four bases—adenine (A), thymine (T), cytosine (C), and guanine (G)—are comprised of hydrogen, carbon, nitrogen and oxygen. (Both cytosine and carbon are symbolized by C, but the context will make clear which is meant.) For the curious, their chemical compositions are: A - $C_5H_5N_5$; T - $C_5H_6N_2O_2$; C - $C_4H_5N_3O$; G - $C_5H_5N_5O$. A and T have two positions to form hydrogen bonds, while C and G have 3 positions; hence, only the base pairs A-T and C-G can form. Hydrogen bonds result from the sharing or transfer of electrons. Each base pair combines with a sugar and a phosphate to form a nucleotide, the basic structural unit of DNA and RNA.

Cells must be replaced regularly. This is accomplished by mitosis, cell division that results in two daughter cells with DNA identical to each other and to the parent DNA. Proteins called cyclins control the cycle of cell division. When not undergoing cell division, DNA is loosely coiled in the nucleus. Prior to mitosis, protein machinery separates the two DNA strands. Working at many different locations on a chromosome, proteins separate the base pairs at a rate of 100/second. Free nucleotides then join the bases to form two identical chromatids that are held together in an X-shape by a centromere; the chromatin has compressed up to 10,000 times. The nuclear membrane disintegrates, and the chromatids line up in a row down the center of the cell. Protein microtubules form a mitotic spindle that attaches to the centromeres to pull the chromatids apart. After nuclear membranes form around the separated chromatids, a contractile ring divides the cell into two identical daughter cells.

Meiosis is cell division of sex cells. The exchange of genetic material during meiosis ensures that no two animals or plants are exactly the same, thus increasing the chances that a species will be able to adapt to change. Fossils show that over time the differences sometimes lead to a new species. In meiosis, after DNA self-replication, pairs of male chromosomes find matching pairs of female chromosomes and exchange gene segments. Cell division follows. A second cell division results in four haploid cells; in humans there are 23 single chromosomes in each sex cell. Swimming up the woman's fallopian tube, the head of a sperm cell penetrates the ovum, delivering 23 single chromosomes to restore the complete set of 23 pairs of chromosomes.

An amazing sequence of events transform a fertilized ovum into an animal. Insects have many stages. A butterfly egg becomes a caterpillar, then chrysalis, before finally emerging as a butterfly. Frog eggs become fishlike tadpoles before they turn into frogs. In amniotes (reptiles, birds and mammals), the animals emerge as adults in miniature. They either crack out of the eggshell or remain inside the mother until birth.

Enzymes begin embryogenesis. In humans, the zygote (fertilized ovum) moves along the fallopian tube to the uterine cavity; cilia lining the tube swish it along. Within 24-36 hours the zygote divides into two, then 4, 8, 16 cells, etc., until the cells are typical body cell size. At this point a ball of embryonic cells called a morula forms. The morula enters the uterine cavity 3-4 days after fertilization. Six days after fertilization a cavity forms around the cell cluster; it is then called a blastocyst. Two days later the blastocyst implants on the endometrium (uterus lining). The inner group of cells, which will become the embryo, includes stem cells that later differentiate into various types of cells such as skin, muscle and nerve cells.

An embryonic disk forms in the inner group of cells, separating the cell cluster into the amniotic cavity, that fills with fluid to cover the embryo, and the yolk sac, that provides nourishment. The disk develops three cell sheets, the endoderm, mesoderm and ectoderm, which are called germ layers. Concentrations of specific proteins in the germ layers instruct the cells where to go to become an arm, leg, etc. The ectoderm curves into a neural tube, which will develop into the spinal cord and brain, and the rest of the body gradually forms from the three germ layers.

A three-weeks-old embryo is 2-3 mm/$^4/_{50}$-$^5/_{50}$" long, with a neural tube, a tube-like heart and a vascular system. The four-weeks-old embryo has a four-chambered heart, simple vessels, lungs, intestines, pancreas, and arm and leg buds. By eight weeks the embryo is 20-30 mm/1-1$^1/_5$" long, with a face, neck, fingers and toes (*Human Body*, 207). It moves. After this, the embryo is a fetus that grows to become a human being, with billions or trillions of cells, 90,000 miles of blood vessels, neurons, senses, limbs, organs, systems, consciousness, the ability to learn, and, eventually, awareness of right and wrong (at least to some degree).

*The Human Body Book*, by Steve Parker, provides illustrations of mitosis, meiosis, embryogenesis, the fetus, and much more. *How We Live and Why We Die*, by Lewis Wolpert, explains cell theory in depth.

We are awed by the wondrous way a single cell develops into a baby, and we cherish the newborn baby, but we often fail to do so with other animals. For example, every year 100 million live male chicks of egg-laying hens in factory farms are ground up or suffocated in plastic bags (peta.org). Underweight piglets are smashed to death against a concrete floor or bashed with a hammer. The will to live is so powerful that a piglet may survive this brutality, to be tossed into a pail, writhing in agony until his or her infant heart ceases to beat. Two-weeks-old baby harp seals are hammered to death or shot. We must extend the scope of our moral responsibility to include nonhuman animals.

Proteins are essential to survival. Because our bodies cannot produce essential amino acids, we must eat protein. However, there is no benefit to consuming animal protein rather than plant protein; in fact, the opposite is true. T. Colin Campbell, an internationally renowned biochemist, devoted his career to studying the relationship between diet and disease. He discovered to his dismay, for he ate animal flesh and dairy, that animal protein consumption correlates with serious afflictions, including cancer, heart disease, autoimmune disorders, osteoporosis, dementia, obesity, diabetes, blindness and more (some of the mechanisms are described later in this book). Plant protein puts one at no such risk, regardless of how much one consumes. Campbell writes about his findings, as well as those of other physicians and scientists, in *The China Study.*

Misinformation and the mistaken assumption, accepted as truth, that it is natural and necessary for people to consume animal flesh and dairy, have been passed from generation to generation, jeopardizing health and leading to abhorrent cruelty to factory farm animals—every year tens of billions of farm animals suffer tremendously before being killed in appalling ways. The livestock sector bears much responsibility for climate change, and our preference for eating animals is bringing about an untold number of extinctions.

## PROTISTS AND INVERTEBRATES

The earliest eukaryotes consisted of mostly unicellular organisms called protists. Protists form the chief part of the plankton drifting in the ocean, providing food for marine life. There are around 30 phyla of protists and more than 100,000 species; in comparison, all vertebrates—mammals, birds, reptiles, amphibians and fish—belong to one phylum, Chordata. Animal-like protists, including amebas, foraminiferans, flagellates, ciliates and many more, are called zooplankton; billions migrate daily up and down the water column. Those with plant characteristics, such as diatoms, are able to photosynthesize; they make up the phytoplankton. Dinoflagellates have characteristics of both plants and animals; zooxanthellae living symbiotically in corals and other marine invertebrates are dinoflagellates. Protists come in myriad different shapes that, magnified, look like they could be made into jewelry. Some, such the dinoflagellate *Noctiluca scintillans*, are bioluminescent, sparkling in the sea at night; chemical reactions within the cytoplasm cause organelles to emit an enchanting blue-green light. Some protists have hard coverings called tests, made of silica or calcium carbonate, while others are soft and can change their shape. Some have arms to catch food particles or tail-like flagella that enable them to swim. Protists are essential to the ocean food web. We share genes with them (supporting the theory of evolution), we share with them the wondrous eukaryotic cell.

There are fossils of multicellular life from 2.1-1.7 billion years ago and fossils from 1.2 billion years ago that show life with differentiated, specialized cells and sexual reproduction. Since then, animals have evolved varied, marvelous solutions to the challenges of life—movement, eating, reproduction and survival.

Sponges are simple sessile animals living on the floor of the sea in coral reefs, rocky reefs and elsewhere. There are 15,000 sponge species, with a variety of shapes, sizes and colors. The barrel sponge grows to 2m/6'. Some species, such as the blue sponge and lemon sponge, are exquisitely colored. Sponges may have tubular, spherical or thread-like forms. They are the only animal species without differentiated tissues and nerve tissue. Sponges have no organs. Collar cells, with flagella that draw in water through pores, line their body, and a ring of tentacles at the end of the flagella trap food; the water and waste leave through larger openings called oscula. Calcareous or glassy spicules throughout the sponge's body support it.

Cnidarians (coelenterates), including corals, anemones, jellyfish and hydroids, appeared around 580 million years ago; there are 8,000 to 9,000 extant species. Reef-building corals and anemones consist of colonies of small sessile animals. Each animal, called a polyp, has a tubular shape with an opening that faces upward. The opening is surrounded by tentacles; cnidocytes (stinging cells) in the tentacles contain barbed threads that shoot out to pierce a prey's skin, then the tentacles bring it in. The polyps multiply by budding; a juvenile identical to the adult grows from its side. There is also sexual reproduction. The reef expands as the polyps multiply. At night corals may attack other corals in order to expand.

Reef-building coral and sea anemone colonies occur in many sizes and shapes. The giant brain coral may reach 2m/ 6.5' and live more than 100 years. Zooxanthellae residing in corals help to sustain the them. Corals secrete exoskeletons of calcium carbonate. Soft corals have spicules of calcium carbonate throughout their tissue. Some soft corals look very like plants. Coral reefs are the habitat of 25% of all marine species; like rain forests, they have amazing biodiversity.

Jellyfish have a body shaped like a saucer or bell that is often transparent. The mouth and tentacles of most species face downward. Tens of thousands of jellyfish can sometimes be seen drifting by together in the sea. Some jellyfish, like the mauve stinger, are bioluminescent and lovely. All cnidarians have a nervous system to sense chemicals and temperature and for touch.

There are 20,000 flatworm species. Their thin bodies consist of a gut and muscles. The candy stripe flatworm and thysanozoon flatworm are beautiful, with convoluted edges that resemble ruffles. The candy-stripe worm has thin stripes on its yellowish body, the thysanozoon worm is black edged with white; yellow-tipped papillae are sprinkled over its body. There are 900 ribbon worm species, some growing to more than 50m/160'! Their anatomy is more complex than that of flatworms, with nerves, blood vessels, ovaries, gut, excretory organs, simple eyes, and a long, sheathed proboscis that shoots out from the mouth to capture prey. The 15,000 species of segmented worms include many marine species. A segmented worm was found in an ocean trench down 8,000m/26,000'. After land plants evolved, the earthworm, a segmented worm, became essential to the soil. The segments (metameres) of a segmented worm, excepting the head and tail tip, are identical, each having blood vessels, a nerve cord, intestine, excretory organ, and parapods on each side for movement. Like flatworms, some segmented worms are beautiful and don't resemble typical worms at all. For example, the magnificent feather duster looks just like its name suggests, with abundant, feathery tentacles. The Christmas tree worm hides in a calcareous tube, extending twin spirals of colorful tentacles.

Bivalves (clams, oysters, mussels), gastropods (slugs and snails), and cephalopods (squid, octopuses and cuttlefish) are mollusks, a phylum with 50,000 species, mostly ocean dwellers, that first appeared 550-530 million years ago.

Mollusks live everywhere from reef beds to the ocean depths; clams and mussels have been found eating a whale carcass on the abyssal plain, down 4,500m/14,800'.

Generally, mollusks have a head, foot and soft body with a hydrostatic skeleton; internal fluid pressure supports the body. A body layer called a mantle covers the upper body. In many species, the mantle secretes a shell. Snails and slugs may have a cone or spiral shell, the bivalve shell has two halves, and cuttlefish have an internal shell called a cuttle. Mollusks have four of the same senses as humans—touch, smell, taste and sight. Some species have no eyes, others have simple eyes along the mantle's edges or siphons, and cephalopods can see color images. The nervous system consists of paired bundles of ganglia. Cephalopods are very intelligent.

Mollusks move in different ways. Slugs and snails move with their foot; a mucus secretion helps them over rocks. Bivalves swim by clapping the halves of their shell. Cephalopods swim, some even have fins. They also move backwards by jet propulsion, squirting water from siphons. Most mollusks have gills for respiration. Hemocyanin transports oxygen in their blood, giving the blood a bluish color.

Mollusks can be either male or female, or hermaphrodite; they may change from one gender to the other. Many species release eggs or sperm into the water, up to 50 million eggs in the case of the giant clam! Cephalopods fertilize internally. The larvae of mollusks form part of the plankton.

The giant octopus is one of the world's most devoted mothers. After depositing up to 100,000 eggs in a safe place, she guards them and regularly squirts water over them to clean them. She does this for 6-8 months, until they hatch. Because she doesn't eat during this time, she dies from starvation after they hatch.

Mollusks come in many sizes, from small snails to the giant cuttlefish (1.5m/5') or the giant octopus (9 m/30'). The giant clam, growing up to 1.5m/5' in diameter, and weighing up to 220kg/440lb., lives on reef flats. Like corals, giant clams rely on zooxanthellae for nourishment. The shell of a giant clam is colorful, often with an iridescent sheen. The flamingo tongue, a reef-dwelling cowrie, has beautiful patterns on its mantle. The Spanish dancer is an elegant nudibranch (shell-less sea slug), beautifully colored in red, pink or orange, sometimes with white trim; it swims in an undulating way that evokes its namesake. The skin of an octopus or cuttlefish changes color, for camouflage and to reflect mood. Some squid, such as firefly squid that live in the ocean depths, are bioluminescent.

Extinct arthropods called trilobites were abundant during the Cambrian 570-510 million years ago. There are more than 1.1 million living arthropod species. Crustaceans, including lobsters, crabs, shrimp, krill and copepods, are ocean-dwelling arthropods; there are 50,000 species (the same number as mollusks). They live nearly everywhere in the ocean, even hydrothermal vents and cold seeps; an amphipod was discovered down 10,911m/35,797' in an ocean trench.

Like land arthropods (insects and spiders), crustaceans have a segmented body. Their exoskeleton may be hardened with calcium carbonate. Adults molt the exoskeleton throughout their lives. Crustaceans have two body segments, a cephalothorax and abdomen. The body cavity has hemolymph rather than blood in the circulatory system. Crustaceans have organs, including heart, stomach, digestive gland and eyes. Their nervous system consists of ganglia. Paired, jointed appendages are used for walking, swimming, or as sensory antennae; some species, like lobsters, have a pair of claws.

The larvae of crustaceans, as well as small crustaceans, form most of the ocean's zooplankton, providing food for all oceanic food chains. Copepods make up more than 70% of the zooplankton. Huge numbers of krill, copepods and other zooplankton travel daily from the ocean depths to the surface waters to feed on plankton. Other crustaceans migrate, too: Caribbean spiny lobsters migrate each winter on the sea floor in search of warmer water, and on Christmas Island millions of red crabs migrate yearly to spawn, traveling from their forest home to the sea in a week-long journey.

Research has established that crustaceans feel pain. The lobster dropped alive into boiling water feels pain (peta.org); it is irrelevant whether the lobster experiences pain in the same way as a human being. To eat animals that are boiled alive is to participate in cruelty.

There are 7,000 echinoderm species, including starfish, sand dollars, sea urchins, feather stars, sea potatoes, sea lilies, sea cucumbers, sea apples and brittlestars. The echinoderm body has a five-star radial symmetry, with an exoskeleton comprised of calcium carbonate; in some species spines extend from the skeleton. Echinoderms can regenerate lost limbs and even a body, as long as the lost limb retains part of it. They have a system of water-filled canals for moving, feeding and respiration. Reservoirs attached to hundreds of tube feet squeeze water in and out. The echinoderm body has a mouth, anus, intestine and gonad. Males and females release sperm and eggs during spawning.

Echinoderms may be grazers, filter feeders, or predators. Crown-of-thorns starfish are large (up to 50cm/20″). Their many arms are covered with long, poisonous spines. The tropical feather star has 100 feathery arms that stand up in the water to catch food; its small body attaches to corals. The red and white passion flower feather star has around 20 arms of different lengths, suggesting a flower. Echinoderms inhabit reefs, the shore and seabed.

Calcium carbonate ($CaCO_3$) is present in most of the exoskeletons of the marine invertebrates described above. Increased carbon dioxide in the sea, from human activity, is leading to ocean acidification, which can dissolve calcium carbonate. Acidification, rising sea levels and warmer ocean temperatures are causing coral reefs to disappear, and with them innumerable animals essential to the ocean food web that have calcium carbonate tests, spicules or exoskeletons. Our diet and lifestyle choices, along with human population growth, are bringing about a tragedy of almost incomprehensible proportions. The longer we deny or ignore climate change, the more serious the consequences.

# FISH

The Age of Fish occurred 418-354 million years ago. Fish are the first vertebrates. Nearly all existing fish species fall into two categories, cartilaginous and bony fish. There are around 1,114 species of cartilaginous fish, including sharks, skates, rays and chimaeras. Cartilage is a firm, flexible tissue less hard than bone; our nose and ears are made of cartilage, and our skeletons are mostly cartilage when we are born, changing to bone as we grow.

Some sharks have large brains and are superb predators. Rows of teeth stand in line to move forward when the ones in the front row are worn out; a tooth may be replaced every week or so. The teeth have hard enamel. They are shaped like needles or daggers, or they may have a serrated edge to slice through fish. Shark skin is tough and feels like sandpaper.

Sharks have a streamlined body, asymmetrical tail, anal, dorsal, pectoral and pelvic fins, and the mouth is often located on the underside. The pectoral fins are winglike in rays; the manta ray has a wingspan of up to 8m/26'! Sharks have eyes similar to those of humans, but instead of eyelids, transparent membranes protect their eyes underwater. They have tiny electrical sense organs dotting their snout that pick up weak electrical signals of other marine life. Most species have a lateral-line system like bony fish, that detects movements in the water. Predatory sharks can smell and taste drops of blood.

Sharks can grow very large. For example, the whale shark reaches up to 20m/65' and can weigh more than 13 tons, and the white shark may reach 7.2m/ 24'. The whale shark is a gentle filter feeder, the white shark a predator. Both roam great distances. Cartilaginous fish lack a swim bladder, but big sharks swimming in the open ocean have a large oil-filled liver that makes them more buoyant. Most sharks and rays have live births after a long gestation; mothers don't care for their newborns.

There are 28,000 species of bony fish, and individual species may occur in great numbers. Bony fish live in fresh water and the sea, from the poles to the tropics. Ocean-dwelling species inhabit shallow seas, open waters, and the ocean depths—basketweave dusk-eels live down 8,000m/ 26,000'. Bony fish have a skull, ribs, backbone, and nearly all species, called ray-finned fish, have spines extending from the backbone to bony rays in the fins. The fins of bony fish are more flexible than those of cartilaginous fish, permitting them to steer and brake and swim backwards. Overlapping scales made of thin bone protect the fish. To aid in buoyancy, bony fish have a swim bladder that fills with gas (usually oxygen) as necessary

Bony fish have the same five senses as humans— sight, hearing, touch, taste and smell. Fish living in shallow waters see in color, whereas those living in the ocean depths have tiny eyes and don't have color vision, relying more on smell and sound. Most bony fish have a lateral line sensory system.

Ray-finned fish release eggs and sperm into the water, where the eggs are fertilized. They may release huge numbers of eggs—the giant ocean sunfish releases 100 million eggs! The eggs hatch into larvae, then transform into juvenile fish, and finally, adults.

Ray-finned fish have an amazing variety of shapes, sizes and colors. Sailfish, ocean sunfish, sand tigers, European sturgeons, conger eels, and northern bluefin tuna all grow to be 3m/10' or larger; the oarfish reaches up to 11m/36'. At the opposite end, the Indonesian cyprinid is only 7-8cm/$^1$/$_3$". Thousands of species have a conventional fish shape, but others don't. Eels have a snake-like body, flounders a flattened body, many reef fish have a thin, deep shape. Some sea dragons look like seaweed. Coral reef fish can be exquisitely patterned with joyous yellows and blues and oranges and whites—the clownfish looks as elegant as a Matisse. Some fish are silvery, others are camouflaged as rocks. Many deep sea fish are bioluminescent.

Small fish often swim in shoals or balls, the great numbers protecting them. Others camouflage themselves to where they're indistinguishable from their surroundings. Flying fish escape predators by using their elongated pectoral and pelvic fins to fly up to 6m/20' above the sea at speeds up to 70kmph/43mph, remaining airborne up to 400m/1,300'! Little gobies in Hawaii climb huge waterfalls to reach the safety above, where they lay their eggs.

Scientists continue to learn about fish intelligence. Stefan Schuster found that an archerfish will observe a skilled archerfish to learn how to shoot a stream of water at a moving target. Archerfish calculate in a fraction of a second where their prey will land after being hit by the stream of water, and they figure out how fast they must swim to reach the prey as it touches the water (*Animal Wise*, 49-64). Researchers have observed mackerel guiding their prey, and groupers lead moray eels to rocks to drive out the fish concealed in the cracks and crevices. Fish learn where to find food and which predators are dangerous. Fish have individual personalities and remarkable memories. The elephant fish has a brain proportionally as large as the human brain!

Scientific studies confirm that fish hooks cause fish pain. Victoria Braithwaite, a fish biologist, discovered that a fish has pain receptors around its mouth; when in pain, the fish rubs the sore spot and acts despondent (*Animal Wise,* 65-73). The evidence that fish hooks make fish suffer brings moral considerations to fishing, as does the threat of extinction to many species targeted by sport fishermen.

Much of the ocean fish population has been fished. Cod and salmon are now mostly farmed. Farm fish are fed wild fish, contributing to the problem. Also, toxic chemicals are used to kill sea-lice on salmon. Factory ships roam the sea, catching immense numbers of fish with nets and longlines that have thousands of fish hooks. Commercial fishermen have begun to fish the deep sea, where fish reproduce very slowly. Some species with great losses in population are the sand eel, Atlantic herring, South American pilchard, Allis shad, Atlantic salmon, Atlantic cod, roughy, northern bluefin tuna, European eel, white shark, piked dogfish, Greenland shark, blue shark and common skate (*Ocean,* 344-71). The European sturgeon and small tooth sawfish are critically endangered, and the frilled shark and bluntnose six-gill shark have lost great numbers.

Countless sharks are caught, their fins sliced off for shark fin soup; they are then tossed back into the sea, wounded and helpless, to die. For every human a shark kills, we kill half a million sharks and more. The good news is that Indonesia and China have begun to take steps to protect sharks and rays, by creating sanctuaries, forbidding shark fishing in some provinces, destroying boats with fins and sharks that were fishing illegally, promoting tourism, and not serving shark fin soup at China state dinners. (*Humane Economy,* 248-9). In October, 2016, CITES declared that fisheries cannot take 9 ray species or the thresher shark until they prove that these fish are sustainable.

A third of the fish caught commercially become animal feed. 25-40% of what is caught is by-kill (cowspiracy.org.)— seabirds, turtles, dolphins, seals, alligators and other marine life become trapped, suffocate, or are tossed overboard, wounded, to die.

The sea, where life on Earth began, is dying. Climate change is causing ocean acidification, rising sea temperatures and sea levels, and deaths of coral reefs. Mangrove swamps and other marine habitats are being destroyed. Waste from nuclear dumping, livestock excrement, toxicants like pesticides, herbicides and chemical fertilizers, plastic bags and other trash fill the sea and destroy marine life. Oil spills pollute the oceans, killing marine life. There is noise pollution, including sonar testing, which brings suffering and death to animals that rely on echolocation. The oceans are crowded with factory ships, speed boats and other ocean vessels that crash/kill marine life. Why desecrate something as magnificent and essential as the sea? Our priorities are askew. May each one of us come to treasure the sea and to express that love in every action, every choice.

Humans have no need to consume fish protein or any animal protein. Cholesterol is present in all animal tissue (however lean/skim), in animal cell membranes, but not in plants. High blood cholesterol is an important predictor of diseases like cancer, heart disease, etc. (*The China Study*, 77). Our bodies produce all the cholesterol we need. Excess cholesterol can build up as plaque in the arteries to restrict the flow of blood and therefore the amount of oxygen delivered to cells. With less oxygen, mitochondria produce less ATP. (In tests comparing a vegan diet to one that includes fish, there may be no distinction made between a whole foods vegan diet and an unhealthy vegan diet, with misleading conclusions.)

One's food choices make all the difference to personal health and to the animals, the Earth. Can the taste of fish or other animal protein be worth the risk of loneliness and depression from dementia? Locked-in syndrome possibly following a stroke? The layers and layers of fat that may build up to impede movement and that often lead to diabetes, with the threat of blindness, heart disease, amputation, etc.? Cancer? Hip replacements made necessary by osteoporosis? Supporting the suffering of animals every purchase of fish or other animal protein? Climate change and the infinite sadness of human-caused mass extinction? Eating an organic vegan diet is crucial to saving life on Earth—the only way to be kind to oneself and to our family of animals.

A human population of over 9 billion, forecast by mid-century, means that there may well be great economic hardship. This doesn't provide an argument to continue large-scale commercial fishing. Beyond the immediate or near future, economic interests dovetail with ethical and environmental concerns. We cannot survive as a species if we continue to destroy/abuse other species. Our arrogance, selfishness and cruelty shame us. There is magnificence in the human spirit; let us access it now!

## PLANTS AND INSECTS AND EARTHWORMS

Two billion years ago animals and plants divided into separate kingdoms. By 580-540 million years ago, an atmospheric ozone layer had formed that screened out enough ultraviolet rays for life on land to be possible. Fungi appeared 560 million years ago (possibly even 1.43 billion years ago). Rather than photosynthesize, they absorb nutrients from organic matter. Fungi called mycorrhizae have a symbiotic relationship with plant roots; they increase the plant's ability to absorb water by up to 1,000 times, while the plant provides them with nutrients.

488-444 million years ago land plants evolved from green algae found by lakes, waterfalls and in other damp places; modern ecosystems appeared 100 million years later. Algae don't have true stems, roots, leaves, or a way to transport sap, but they contain chlorophyll, a green pigment that absorbs sunlight during photosynthesis. The sun's energy is used to synthesize food from carbon dioxide and water, with oxygen as a byproduct.

A plant cell consists of cytoplasm, where organelles such as chloroplasts (distant relatives of cyanobacteria), proteins and mitochondria are found, and a nucleus containing

DNA. Plant cells differ from animal cells in some ways. A boxlike cell wall made up of cellulose (molecules of sugar bonded together) encloses the protoplasm. In vascular plants, sap, composed of water with dissolved sugar and minerals, is transported in the plant's vascular system. The genome of a plant can be as large or larger than the human genome; for instance, the human genome has 22,000 genes and around 3 billion nucleotides, while the wheat genome has 25,000 genes and 16 billion nucleotides.

Chlorophyll, present in the chloroplasts of plant cells, contains proteins that absorb light energy. Light energy, with water and carbon dioxide, is involved in chemical reactions that produce oxygen, ATP and nicotinamide adenine dinucleotide phosphate (NADPH). Light provides the energy for $CO_2$ to be added to carbon compounds such as ribulose diphosphate. ATP and NADPH help convert the resulting compounds into glucose and other carbohydrates that are food sources for animals. During digestion, mitochondria in animal cells use glucose and oxygen to produce ATP, with $CO_2$ as a byproduct, in a remarkable reciprocity with plants.

Communication between cells in plants is similar to that of animals; calcium ions play an important role in neural communication in both plants and animals, and both use glutamate receptors. Myosin, important in muscle movement of animals, helps plants to absorb water and minerals. Plants, like animals, feel gravity and are aware of the time of day. Plants sometimes help each other. A tree may provide its saplings with nutrients, and sometimes a tree will do the same for a tree of another species. *What a Plant Knows,* by Daniel Chamovitz, describes this recent research concerning plants.

The first plants, such as liverworts and mosses, were small and lacked true roots. 430-420 million years ago vascular plants appeared, and over the next 70 million years land plants developed seeds, leaves and roots. Wood evolved. During this time, marine animals, including microscopic bacteria and protists such as amebas and flagellates, ancestral velvet worms, mollusks such as snails and slugs, horseshoe crabs, and arachnids like scorpions, began to explore the new land habitats. The protective exoskeletons many had evolved in the sea helped them to retain water on land.

Over millions of years a wonderful relationship developed between plants and invertebrates and microorganisms. Plants supply food, while soil inhabitants create a loamy soil in which plants thrive. Earthworms surface at night to take dead leaves underground. They eat dirt, transforming it into particles of different sizes, making porous soil that is able to hold air and water. Microorganisms, insects, worms, millipedes and other soil inhabitants break down decaying leaves and other plant matter into humus. Humus provides a microscopic edifice that stores water and lets microbes thrive. It retains nutrients such as calcium, potassium, phosphorus, magnesium and iron, that otherwise might drain away in rains. Microorganisms use nitrogen in producing organic compounds that feed plants.

Around 400 million years ago, as plants flourished on land, insects appeared. There are over one million known insect species, perhaps millions more yet to be discovered. Insects are small arthropods with six hinged legs and an exoskeleton made of chitin. Chitin is a carbohydrate like starch or cellulose; the tracheae that deliver oxygen to an insect's tissues are also comprised of chitin. The insect body has three segments—a head, thorax, to which legs and wings are attached, and abdomen. There is almost limitless variety within this basic design. Hemolymph, rather than blood, circulates through the insect's body cavity. Many insect species have large compound eyes; some have eyes at the ends of stalks. Though they have ganglia instead of a brain, insects are able to learn and remember. Insects such as the stick insect are superbly camouflaged. Other insects protect themselves with a venomous sting, or they may spray formic acid (made from carbon monoxide and steam). Insects can be beautiful—there is a splendid array of colors in the insect world, and no animal is more lovely than a butterfly.

Springtails, among the most ancient insects, appeared 395 million years ago. They have established themselves everywhere and in great numbers—up to 10,000/square meter. A springtail measures less than 5mm/0.2″, yet a two-pronged lever under its abdomen permits it to leap six inches—30 times its body size—above the leaf litter! Two inflatable tubes provide a waterproofing fluid which the springtail applies over its body to keep moist. The female chooses a mate who best opposes her in head-to-head confrontation. The couple dances, the male twirls at the dance's conclusion, and sperm is deposited.

Plants grew taller. Forests of conifers spread across the land. Around 350 million years ago, the exoskeletons of many insect species transformed into wings. There are fossils of ancient dragonflies that have a wingspan of two-and-a-half feet. Dragonflies can fly up to 65kmph/40 mph. They have two sets of wings; their wings move independently, so they are able to fly in any direction or hover. Once their wings unfold, they never close. Dragonflies take to the air only at the end of their lives, following a five-year larval stage.

Beetles appeared around 280 million years ago. They have been enormously successful, with some 300,000 extant species in myriad sizes and shapes. Their forewings became hard wing cases (elytra) to protect the hind wings.

By 200 million years ago, forests of conifers, cycads and ginkgoes were established. Sequoias, modern-day conifers, are the tallest trees, reaching 110m/325'. 5,000-year-old coniferous bristlecone pines can be found in mountainous regions of western North America.

160-120 million years ago flowering plants (angiosperms) appeared; there are now 250,000-400,000 species. Angiosperms need pollinators. To attract insects and birds, many species have perfumed flowers and nectar. The nectar of some flowers is deep within the flower, and some insect species evolved special anatomical features in order to access it. For example, the lower jaws of a butterfly are long and thin. Tiny hooks lining the inner edges zip together, forming a coiled tube. Muscles and nerves cause the tube to uncurl. After the butterfly sips nectar, elastic resilin in the tube (formed of cross-linked protein chains) lets it recoil.

Butterflies first appeared 190 million years ago, and modern-day species evolved 40 million years ago. There are around 15,000 existing species. Two pairs of overlapping wings, made up of scales, move together as a butterfly flutters. The wing colors are either chemical pigments, or light reflected on the scales, creating iridescent hues. Distinctive colors and patterns help butterflies to recognize each other; orange or red alerts predators that the butterfly is poisonous.

Males flaunt their wings to females during the mating season. The female butterfly deposits her eggs on leaves, where they develop into caterpillars. The caterpillar has a segmented body resembling some types of worms and three pairs of legs, as well as several pairs of appendages that look like legs. The caterpillar molts 5 times, becoming 800 times heavier. It then transforms into a chrysalis, emerging around two weeks later as a butterfly.

Every year a billion monarch butterflies have journeyed some 2,500 miles, from the northeastern United States and Canada to California and Mexico, to hibernate over the winter. The last few years 30 million or less have migrated, and the number continues to decline, though because of conservation efforts, they have begun to rebound a little. Monarchs lay their eggs only on milkweed, which contains a poison the caterpillars consume to protect them when they become butterflies. A widely used weedkiller, glyphosate (marketed as Roundup by Monsanto) kills milkweed. In addition, genetically modified corn pollen dusting the milkweed kills the caterpillars. Genetically modified seeds are designed to withstand herbicides; there has been a tenfold increase of herbicides in recent years, destroying pollinators as well as plants.

Three winters ago I came upon a dead monarch butterfly while walking in an early December snowstorm; it had misjudged the timing of its migration, as is increasingly likely with climate change. Its wings were exquisite—translucent orange framed by black lines that evoke stained glass windows, with white dots sprinkled along the edges. As I held its body, I grieved, remembering the magical time every summer during my childhood when monarchs graced our garden. www.saveourmonarchs.org is dedicated to replanting milkweed.

Pollinators such as bees form colonies of hundreds, thousands, even tens of thousands of individuals. Bees appeared 100 million years ago. They transform nectar into honey in their stomachs, then store it in honeycombs. The queen lays eggs, while sterile females are worker bees.

During her six-week lifespan, a worker bee knows exactly what tasks to perform and when to do so. Her first week she is a cleaner, later a nursemaid, cell-builder, shelf-stacker packing pollen and honey into honeycomb cells, guard, and finally, a collector of nectar and pollen. When a bee returns to the colony after locating a good food source, she tells her sisters how to find it by performing a waggle dance of short, quick movements that informs them of the direction and distance to the flowers. Bees can distinguish between people's faces, as well as understand some abstractions (*Animal Wise*, 35).

Pollinators pollinate one third of foods consumed in the United States, including apples, almonds, avocados, blueberries, broccoli, carrots, cauliflower, cherries, cucumbers, raspberries and sunflowers. Bee colonies are collapsing from the use of pesticides, habitat loss, pests (especially an Asian mite, *Varroa destructor)* and pathogens. Specifically, insecticides called neonicotinoids are devastating bees. Unable to groom themselves, mites take over their bodies, they become ill, their immune systems don't function well, they die. They become lost, disoriented, confused to where they can't return to the colony with food. If they do happen to return, the entire colony is poisoned with the contaminated pollen. In addition, glyphosate decreases sperm count in drones. Some bee species have recently been added to the Endangered Species list.


Ants, that first appeared 80 million years ago, form societies that sometimes include thousands or millions of ants. Morrell writes about the study of tiny rock ants by the British scientist Nigel Franks (*Animal Wise,* 27-48). After finding a new home with exact specifications down to the millimeter, a scout teaches several other ants the route. The remaining ants are then carried to their new home.

Working together, plants and pollinators and other insects are central to land ecosystems. All animals require plants directly or indirectly to survive. Insectivores, including many bird, mammal and reptile species, consume insects and thus help to control insect populations. As we destroy plants and pollinators, we destroy ecosystems that evolved over hundreds of millions of years. Up to half of all plant species may face extinction in the coming century from climate change, deforestation, and annihilation of pollinators; the extinctions will continue for hundreds or thousands of years unless we change. Our diet and lifestyle choices, human population growth and harmful agricultural practices bear responsibility.

In organic farming, earthworms till the soil, and the plants aren't genetically modified to withstand herbicides. An organic vegan diet requires far less land the does an animal-based diet—much deforestation, especially in South America, is to provide grazing land. Organic farming stores carbon in the soil. Soils where pesticides, herbicides and chemical fertilizers are used have lost 50-70% of the carbon they once stored, from flooding, erosion, destruction of the earthworms and microorganisms that decompose vegetative matter, and from transforming grasslands into cropland.

A spiral of climate change and extinction has been set in motion. In this context, the choice to eat an organic vegan diet, or to buy genetically-modified fruits, vegetables, legumes and grains grown with pesticides, herbicides and synthetic chemical fertilizers, and to eat animal-based meals, becomes a matter of life-or-death/extinction.

Plants grown using toxicant/intensive agricultural practices are usually less expensive than organically grown ones, in part because of government subsidies, but the cost to nature is absolutely devastating. Manufacturing and operation of machinery to till the soil use fossil fuels. Invertebrates and protists living in the soil are often destroyed by tilling, and so the plants are deprived of nutrients. The soil can't hold water or air; calcium, phosphorus, iron, etc., are leached away in rains. Synthetic chemical fertilizers make the soil too acidic for earthworms to thrive. When washed into rivers, lakes and the sea, the ammonia fertilizers cause eutrophication, leading to huge die-offs of fish and amphibians and their natural predators. Pesticides and herbicides poison both aquatic life and the wildlife that consume fish, frogs, etc.; herons, raptors and sea birds are threatened. When grocery shopping and voting, remember to honor the environment and life on Earth.

## FROGS

The sound of frogs croaking on summer nights entranced me in childhood. Now, when walking along the river in Zion, I encounter delightful little desert toads. They bravely struggle in the grass, gigantic to them, and frequently they need to right themselves after landing upside down.

The first amphibians appeared 375 million years ago, and frogs evolved 265 million years ago. There are now 4,800 recorded frog species, 88% of all amphibian species. They live in water, trees, ground and burrows, especially in tropical rain forests. Frogs dwelling in colder climates survive when their bodies freeze because high levels of glucose in the vital organs prevent damage. Desert toads burrow beneath the sand for long periods, even years, to surface and breed when the rains come.

Frogs range in size from the 0.76cm/0.3″ *Paedophryne amauensis* frog found in New Guinea, to the goliath frog of Cameroon, which measures 300mm/12″. Frogs live up to 40 years in captivity. The frog skull became heavier than a fish skull, and skeletal adaptations, for example, the enlargement of the spinal cord near places where the limbs attach, made movement on land possible. Their long, strong hind limbs make frogs spectacular jumpers—the Australian rocket frog leaps 50 times its body length! The one-inch waterfall toad free-falls from a tree to escape a predator; its feet have membranes that serve as parachutes. Frogs have many other adaptations to survive on land as well as in water: the head moves sideways to detect prey; the cerebral cortex has more nerve cells than does that of a fish; and changes in the middle ear enable frogs to hear sounds on land.

Frogs have large, bulging eyes placed high on each side, near the top of the head; this gives them stereoscopic vision of 100 degrees, and they can see nearly completely around them. One of three eyelid membranes is transparent, protecting their eyes underwater. The eyes retract through holes in the skull to push food down the throat.

Frogs have small lungs; their skin is also a respiratory organ. They can survive without lungs, and one species, the Borneo flat-headed frog, has no lungs. Frogs have smooth, moist skin or drier, warty skin; those with warty skin are usually called toads. A sticky secretion helps keep the skin moist. Terrestrial species have antibiotic substances in their skin; the skin is very permeable to water. The skin of water-dwelling frogs is less permeable and must kept moist. Frogs are unable to live in sea water. Glands in the skin may secrete distasteful or poisonous substances. The frog sheds its skin every few weeks. Skin may provide camouflage or be brightly colored to alert predators that the frog is poisonous. The skin may darken in cool, damp places, for the frog to absorb as much warmth as possible.

A male frog croaks to find a mate and to stave off predators. Seductive pheromones are secreted. During mating, the male ejects semen from his cloaca onto the female's eggs, climbing on her back and wrapping his forelimbs around her to accomplish this. The eggs do not have a shell, therefore frogs must lay their eggs in water. A gelatinous material surrounds the fetus to nourish and protect it. Oxygen, carbon dioxide and ammonia can pass through. Dark brown or black colors help the eggs to absorb the sun's warmth.

Aquatic tadpoles with front limbs emerge from the eggs. This phase lasts from a week to one or more winters. The oval body and vertically flattened tail are designed for swimming. Tadpoles retain fish characteristics such as gills and a lateral line system. Being herbivorous, they have a lengthy intestine.

Frogs may watch over the eggs and help the tadpoles. Tadpoles of some marsupial frog species find their way to the male's pouches, where they remain safely inside until they metamorphose into frogs. The male Darwin's frog carries the fertilized eggs in his vocal sac for 7-10 weeks, until metamorphosis. The male poison arrow frog carries his tadpoles one by one to water pools in bromeliads in the rainforest canopy; he then prompts a female to deposit an unfertilized egg in each pool to nourish the tadpole. After this, the couple hug frog fashion. A male giant African bullfrog watches over the tadpoles of many bullfrogs, digging a channel to a larger pool should the small pool where the tadpoles are swimming start to dry up.

Thyroxine sets metamorphosis in motion; within 24 hours a tadpole changes into a frog. The gills disappear, lungs develop. Carnivorous anatomical features (including a big mandible, long, sticky cleft tongue, and soft upper teeth to grip prey), digestive organs and kidneys appear. The intestine shortens. The nervous system changes to allow hearing on land and binocular vision. Eyes are relocated higher, eye lids form, the eardrum, middle ear and inner ear develop. The lateral line disappears, the skin toughens and thickens, skin glands develop. The long tail vanishes and limbs grow. A brain, spinal cord and nerves develop.

Frogs are crucial to many food webs around the world. They feed on insects and small animals, and they themselves are food for larger animals. More than one third of frog species are threatened. In addition to annihilating them, human activity is causing sickness, genetic mutations and deformities in frogs—frogs may develop extra limbs or change gender. A terrible fungal disease called chytridiomycosis and other diseases and parasites are decimating them.

Causes of these tragedies include habitat loss, heavy traffic through their habitat, pollutants, climate change, increased UVB radiation, introduction of non-native predators and competitors. Habitat loss and heavy traffic result from human population growth, an animal-based diet and an unsustainable consumer lifestyle. Toxicants such as pesticides, herbicides and chemical fertilizers, washed by rains into rivers and ponds, poison frogs. Carelessly discarded trash, including birth control medications, affect the gender of frogs and cause malformations. Droughts, more frequent with climate change, dry out ponds, killing frogs. Nitrous oxide ($N_2O$) contributes to ozone depletion, which destroys frogs. $N_2O$ is also a major greenhouse gas; livestock waste handling produces much nitrous oxide.

Choices that respect all life are best for us as well: ozone depletion is linked to a greater risk of skin cancer, and climate change has catastrophic consequences. Animal-based diets and toxicant/intensive agriculture harm humans as well as frogs. Money and taste preferences for animals and dairy have taken priority over concern for all life. Our choices, which now ravage other species, will boomerang on humanity, causing immense suffering and great economic cost. And what right do we have to crowd out innumerable other species? We must change course now.

There is some good news regarding chytridiomycosis. In 2007 scientists found that an application of probiotic bacteria helps to protect the skin of frogs from the disease. Conservationists are working incredibly hard to rescue frogs and other endangered animals and plants from extinction, but everyone needs to join in. Each person is responsible to some degree for the crisis. One can help first and foremost by adapting an organic vegan diet, then by foregoing lifestyle choices that involve unsustainable use of resources. The United States uses far more resources than most other countries. We must act responsibly and lead in global efforts to save life on Earth. Donate, volunteer, and perhaps choose a vocation in conservation. Let summer evenings once again fill with the sound of frogs croaking, as they have for hundreds of millions of years. They're our friends, our family, and they urgently need our help.

# REPTILES

Reptile fossils date back 340 million years. The Age of Reptiles, when reptiles dominated the Earth, lasted for more than 200 million years, from 280 to 65 million years ago. Dinosaurs reigned for over 100 million years, until they were annihilated by an asteroid striking the Yucatan Peninsula in Mexico 65 million years ago. Some dinosaurs reached up to 40m/130', though others were much smaller. There were both carnivorous and herbivorous species. Tyrannosaurs and other species were bipedal. Some dinosaurs may have been endothermic (warm-blooded).

Reptiles have adaptations that free them from the need to be near water. Keratinous scales cover their bodies, waterproofing their skin while keeping heat and water in. They are amniotes—the reptile embryo develops within a semi-permeable shell that has several membranes. They either lay their eggs on land or give birth to live animals that look like miniature adults. Reptiles have smaller heads than amphibians. Excepting snakes, that are legless, their limbs are at their side, forming a right angle. Reptiles are ectothermic, meaning they must warm/cool their bodies from external sources like the sun or shade. They need only 10% of the energy mammals require, and they can go days or months between meals.

Modern-day reptiles include lizards, snakes, crocodilians and turtles. Turtles and tortoises have existed since before the Age of the Dinosaurs. They can live 150 years and more; a captive Aldabra giant tortoise lived to be 255 years old! Scales and skeleton are modified into an armored shell that protects a turtle from most predators except humans. The sea turtle has a soft, streamlined shell, enabling it to hide beneath the sand and mud while breathing through its skin and throat lining. A sea turtle's front flippers are like paddles. A sea turtle may journey 1,000km/600mi to lay its eggs on the island beach where it, too, hatched. Leatherback turtles, up to 1.8m/6' long and weighing up to 900kg/2,000lb, are the largest of all marine turtles. They roam thousands of miles at sea and dive down as deep as 1,000m/3,300′. They are equipped with backward-facing throat spines that keep jellyfish, a favorite food, from escaping. Mistaking discarded plastic bags for jellyfish, they swallow them, often dying. They are in danger of extinction, as are most turtles—turtle numbers have declined 80% in recent decades (*The Guardian*, September 30, 2014). For example, the hawksbill turtle's shell is the primary source for tortoiseshell, and young turtles are also killed to be stuffed then sold as tourist curios. In consequence, hawksbills are critically endangered. I have encountered two endangered desert tortoises near Zion. It was an extraordinary experience to see them. They were simple, dignified, moving slowly and peacefully. They are to be treasured, yet they are likely to disappear because of human activity.

The Florida gopher tortoise highlights species interdependence. It digs down 17m/50′ to escape the heat and brush fires. Its burrow provides safety for 100 other species, such as raccoons, rats, rabbits and rattlesnakes, possums and lizards. In another example, African helmeted turtles clean parasites off rhinos and hippos.

Crocodilians include caimans, gharials, alligators and crocodiles. There are a total of 23 species. The saltwater crocodile is the largest reptile, sometimes reaching 8m/26′

and weighing up to 900kg/2,000lb or more. Crocodilians have a strong armor made of scales; some have scutes along their spine that function as solar panels. They continually replace their teeth—they may have 40 sets of teeth during a lifetime. They have muscle flaps that close over their nostrils and ears when diving, and they have another at the top of the throat to prevent the lungs from being flooded when the mouth opens underwater. Waterproof, transparent coverings protect the eyes. Eyes and nostrils are set high on the head; when hunting, the body remains concealed under water. A crocodilian uses its tail to propel itself in water.

Crocodilians can be tender, and some take care of their young. The huge male saltwater crocodile is gentle and affectionate when mating. The female Nile crocodile guards her eggs, helps the newborn crocodiles to break through the shell when necessary, then carries them to water. Sometimes one female crocodile watches over a group of numerous baby crocodiles from different mothers, guarding them, guiding them to water, even when the water is far away.

Crocodilians that live near coral reefs and in mangrove swamps face extinction as the reefs die and the mangrove forests are destroyed. They are killed when they become entangled in fishing nets, from collisions with boats, and from being hunted for their flesh and skin—alligator shoes mean more to us than alligators.

There are 2,718 snake species. Snakes have a flexible backbone, with up to 400 vertebrae. Though legless, they can climb trees, inch forward in a straight line, sidewind in a series of S-shaped curves, (they may lift loops of their body clear off the sand when moving sideways on dunes), swim and glide. Flying snakes stretch out their body, while flattening the underside, to glide through the air. Many snakes have beautifully patterned scales. As they grow, they must shed/replace their skin. Some snakes grow remarkably long—the anaconda may reach 7.2m/25', the Burmese python 7m/23'.

Snakes are carnivorous. Their jaws are loosely joined to each other and to their skull. A ligament connecting the lower jaws allows the jaws to move sideways as well as up and down and to open wide enough to swallow prey whole; an anaconda can swallow a 6-foot caiman, a python can swallow an antelope. A snake tongue is forked. As it flicks in and out, it collects molecules from the air and earth, which are transferred to a sensory organ for smell and taste called Jacobson's organ, located on the roof of the snake's mouth. The information the tongue receives helps the snake track prey, sample food, find a mate, and avoid predators. Pit vipers and rattlers also have heat sensor pits between their nostrils and eyes that locate prey at night. Venomous snakes have specialized teeth called fangs that have a tube within the tooth and a hole at the tip. Venom, used to subdue prey, is stored in a sac against the roof of the mouth. Boa constrictors squeeze their prey to death. After swallowing the prey, the snake's skin stretches to accommodate the body. Stomach and liver enlarge during digestion, which takes up to a week. Egg-eating snakes have a light skull, a mouth lined with sticky ridges to grip the egg, stretchable scales, toothlike spines on the underside of the neck vertebrae to break the shell, and a valve at the stomach entrance to keep out shell pieces, which are regurgitated.

Snakes are the most endangered reptiles, from habitat loss and hunting. The rain forests, habitat for numerous species, are being destroyed. Ocean acidification threatens coral reefs, habitat of sea kraits and other sea snakes. Human development is eliminating the habitat of many desert species. People kill snakes to make snakeskin shoes, purses and belts; as is true regarding crocodilians, these items are more important to us than snakes—what does this say of our values?

Lizards have existed for 340 million years. They usually have a long body and tail. Lizards have four legs, attached to the side of their body rather than beneath it, movable eyelids, and scaly or spiny skin. Lizards can shed their tail to escape danger. Some tails are blue, to distract predators away from the lizard's body.

Monitor lizards are large lizards that inhabit the Old World tropics; the water monitor reaches a length of 2.7m/ 9′. Monitors have a long neck, forked tongue, sharp claws, short body and a narrow head. They are intelligent, equipped with excellent senses, and they are able to chase prey at 20mph for long periods. A long throat pumps air into the lungs. The Komodo dragon, a monitor lizard reaching up to 3m/10′, is able to swallow a water buffalo. Komodo dragons are remarkably smart. Some in captivity have been observed to count. They are curious, and they enjoy being stroked. Captive Komodo dragons play with zookeepers; they recognize different voices, run, climb, swim, dig. They adapt to new situations, using new opportunities to their advantage. Hunting, deforestation and scrub clearing threaten their survival.

The bright green basilisk lizard has feet with broad soles that enable it to walk on water, and so it has been nicknamed the "Jesus Christ" lizard. When escaping a raptor, it runs on its hind legs on water at a speed equivalent to a human running 105kmph/65mph! Geckos are nocturnal lizards that live in warm climates. Adhesive pads on their feet, with hooked ridges, allow them to move vertically on smooth surfaces. The pygmy gecko is light enough to walk on water.

Iguanas are large lizards living in trees of the New World tropics. They are green, with a spiny crest along their back. Marine iguanas in the Galapagos Islands are the only herbivores among lizards, as well as the only marine lizards.

Chameleons are Old World lizards that change their skin color to camouflage, display, or to reflect their mood. Their eyes rotate independently. Toes divide into groups of three and two, forming pincers to grip branches. The tail is prehensile. Chameleons have an inflatable throat flap. A spectacularly long tongue shoots out to catch unsuspecting insects.

Shingleback lizards, found in Australian deserts, form bonds that can last for two decades. They stay close to each other during the two-month mating season. Shinglebacks like to warm up on highways. When a car crushes one, the mate will remain beside the body for days, seeming to grieve.

Horned lizards inhabit the southwestern United States. They were common in my childhood, but have become rare, from being captured for the exotic pet trade. Our venerable reptilian relatives, with whom we share DNA, the eukaryotic cell, tissues, organs and systems, are in peril because of us— our selfishness and species arrogance. We must come to their rescue!

# BIRDS

Zion National Park is home or migratory stopover for over 200 bird species. Wild turkeys contentedly forage together, their feathers lovely iridescent gold, teal and bronze hues. Bluebirds and yellow warblers give bursts of happiness as they fly by. A mother duck and her ducklings sweetly glide down the river, elegantly patterned woodpeckers make tree holes, peregrine falcons dive, and ravens, hawks and eagles soar above the cliffs. A lone blue heron calmly fishes, colorful summer tanagers and towhees and orioles and grosbeaks stay for a time. The air fills with the songs of canyon wrens, warblers and other birds. To watch birds go about their daily lives gives me the keenest pleasure.

Birds are living representatives of dinosaurs. In 2000 Chinese scientists described finding fossils of a small dinosaur called a micro-raptor that had some feathers—a transitional fossil ancestor to birds. *Archaeopteryx* (Greek for "ancient wing"), a 147-million-year-old fossil discovered in

Germany, is believed to have been the first bird. It was like a dinosaur in having a heavy skull, long bony tail, claws and teeth, and lacking a deep breastbone, but it had the feathers and hollow bones of birds. Its skeleton is the size of a pigeon's.

There are close to 10,000 existing bird species. Birds have up to 25,000 feathers. Feathers, like hair, nails, horns, scales, hoofs, claws and baleen, are made of keratin. A feather has a shaft, with vanes on either side composed of barbs and overlapping barbules that keep the barbs in place. Short, soft, downy feathers insulate a bird, even in extreme cold (-31°C/-35°F). Longer contour feathers form a smooth cover over the bird's body, wing and tail feathers permit flight, and covert feathers cover the bases of the wing and tail feathers. Birds replace their feathers at least once a year.

To be light enough to fly, birds evolved hollow bones, with struts for support. Wing bones correspond to the human arm; the bend is the location of the wrist, and from there to the wing tip are hand and finger bones. Powerful muscles attached to the bird's breastbone, with a ligament over the shoulder blade functioning as a pulley, move the wings up and down. Flight requires energy. To maximize the amount of oxygen in their cells, birds have, in addition to lungs, an average of nine air sacs within their bodies. Nearly all the oxygen is replaced every breath.

Birds have remarkable variations in size, wing shape, and the ways and length of time they fly. Hummingbirds, only a few inches long, beat their tiny wings up to 80 times a second as they move up, down, backwards, forwards, or hover to sip nectar. Songbirds have short, rounded wings to take off quickly and maneuver easily among trees. Raptors spread their large, broad wings to soar up thermals, glide in the high sky searching for prey, then dive to capture prey with their talons. The peregrine falcon dives at a speed of 193kmph/120mph or faster (it is difficult to clock the speed precisely). The Ruppell's vulture climbs to 11,000m/33,000'. The albatross has long, slender wings to soar over the ocean; it may remain airborne for months at a time. The sooty tern stays in the sky for the first 8-9 years of its life, even sleeping on the wing. Penguin wings are used as flippers.

Birds have superb color vision. They recognize each other by the color and patterns of their plumage, to our immeasurable good fortune: the bright, joyful reds, blues, greens and yellows of parrots; the vivid red of the scarlet tanagers and cardinals; the thrilling blue of bluebirds; the emerald green of the resplendent quetzal; the vibrant deep orange of a flame robin; the cheerful yellow of American yellow warblers; the iridescent jewel tones of hummingbirds; the artistic black and white designs of loons.

Males are often more colorful than females, especially during mating season. None is more splendid than the Indian peacock, with around 200 long, elegant covert tail feathers that stand upright and fan out in display. The scarlet tanager adopts red plumage during the mating season; in winter its plumage is yellow.

The spatuletail hummingbird shows off his long tail by dancing in the air before a female. Some male birds serenade females with exquisite songs. The bower bird spends years creating a beautiful space to seduce females. A million lesser flamingos gather during the mating season at Lake Bogota, joining in promenades of a thousand to find a mate. Birds may preen each other and offer food to one another during courtship. Most bird species are monogamous, from one nesting to life. Grebes, that mate for life, perform exquisite dances together every spring to affirm their bond.

Many birds migrate long distances in search of food and a safe place to breed. Arctic terns zigzag 44,000 miles a year between Greenland and Antarctica. Red knots travel from northern Alaska to the tip of South America and back every year, a roundtrip of over 30,000km/18,600mi. Geese, ducks, cranes, rufous hummingbirds and other birds migrate hundreds to thousands of miles yearly. Migratory birds use a star chart to guide them. They adjust their direction to correct for the Earth's declination and for the change in the night sky as the seasons and their latitudinal positions change. Microscopic specks of magnetite sensitize migratory birds to the geomagnetic field. They may also memorize the coastline.

A bird's physiology and anatomy correspond to its diet. The bill, made of bone covered with keratin, is a feeding tool designed in various ways. The toucan's fabulous bill allows it to reach otherwise inaccessible fruit. The hooked beak of a raptor tears the flesh after the bird has killed the animal with its talons. The sword-billed hummingbird has a slender bill about as long as its body, with which it sucks nectar from flowers that have long tubular corollas. The long curved bill of the curlew reaches deep into mud to retrieve worms. The curved bill of a flamingo has lamellae (fibrous-edged plates) that filter insects, worms and algae from water; flamingos feed with their bill upside down. Pelicans have the biggest beaks—50cm/18.5" long—with mandibles that bow out when the pelican's pouch fills with water. The heron and egret spear fish with their sharp pointed bills.

Bills have functions beyond feeding, such as recognition and building nests. Some birds use their beaks to hold tools. The woodpecker finch holds a cactus spine in its beak, using the needle-like spine to access insects hidden in crevices. Crows make tools. In experiments, a captive crow named Betty understood that a hooked wire made it easier to retrieve a bucket of food, and she taught herself to make a hook. Lammergeiers (bearded vultures) in Ethiopia eat bone marrow. They drop large bones onto rocks to smash the bones open, in order to access the marrow. Oystercatchers hammer mollusk shells open on rocks. The green heron uses insects and earthworms to bait minnows. A woodpecker stores up to 30,000 acorns, drilling a space for each one in tree bark with its beak.

Birds are intelligent. A scrub jay will return to relocate his cache of seeds at a later time if he notices another bird observing him when he first stashes his food. Crows make 250 different calls and recognize each other's individual voices. African grey parrots are among the most intelligent birds. N'kisi, an African grey parrot living with Aimee Morgana, developed a vocabulary of over a thousand words. Ms. Morgana once showed N'kisi a video of Jane Goodall, but never taught him the word 'chimp'. Still, when he met Dr. Goodall, he exclaimed, "chimp lady!" N'kisi seemed to be telepathic. To test this, he and Ms. Morgana were placed in locked rooms 50 feet a part. He accurately described 23 of the 71 photographs Ms. Morgana was shown.

Alex, another grey parrot, taught himself to say "calm down" when his human friend, Irene Pepperberg, was stressed. He understood what "none" meant and that the number 6 was equivalent to six objects, also that the number 6 was greater than five objects. He comprehended when objects were the same or different. And he was smart enough to grow impatient with the repetitive tests he was forced to endure to prove his intelligence to humans.

Scientists are observing in birds and other animals much that we had mistakenly believed to be uniquely human—signature calls equivalent to names, self-awareness, abstract thought, planning for the future, culture, empathy, kindness, laughter, grieving, suffering. This knowledge is removing any rationale for anthropocentric arrogance, bringing into focus our cruelty to our nonhuman family.

Bird legs and feet vary depending on the bird's diet and lifestyle. Herons have long legs to stand in water while fishing. Waterfowl such as ducks have webbed or lobed feet. Passerines like songbirds have four toes, one or two of them opposable, for gripping a branch or twig. Eagles and other raptors have talons to capture prey.

More than two-thirds of all bird species eat animals. Raptors and owls prey on birds and mammals, vultures are scavengers, seabirds catch fish and invertebrates, other species consume insects and/or earthworms. Plant-eating species eat seeds, flowers and/or pollen, or they sip nectar. Some birds are omnivores.

The digestive system of each bird species is suited to its diet. Food may first be stored in the crop, located in front of the wishbone. During digestion, the proventriculus (upper part of the stomach) secretes acids that break down animal protein and turn seeds and flowers into pulp; it is larger in birds of prey and carrion eaters. The gizzard (lower part of the stomach) is larger in plant-eating birds. Muscles in the gizzard churn the food. Sometimes a bird swallows grit to aid in digestion.

Birds take care to find a safe breeding place. Birds are amniotes like mammals and reptiles. The fertilized eggs are incubated by one or both parents. Male emperor penguins shelter eggs on top of their feet, beneath a fold of skin, during the Antarctic winter. Some birds lay their eggs on the ground or make nests from mud. Weavers create lovely nests by weaving strips of grass and reeds together; some add a three-foot long entrance tunnel to keep out predators. Bald eagles return to the same nest every year. Many generations may use the same nest, until it becomes huge—one measured 3 m/10′ wide and 6m/19.5′ deep!

The process by which a bird's fertilized egg becomes a nestling is similar to the way a fertilized human egg becomes a baby. Once the nestlings have hatched, the parents often go to great effort to feed them. Songbirds make around 2,000 trips a day to bring food to their nestlings. Atlantic puffins and chinstrap penguins travel 50 miles and more to find food for their newborns. The chinstrap penguins and rockhopper penguins, despite having bodies designed to move in water, climb steep cliffs to breed/feed their young in safe locations, an enormously challenging act of parental devotion.

The backyard of a house where I once lived was adjacent to a yard with four chickens that would fly over the wall to visit. We single out two bird species—domestic chickens and turkeys—for unimaginable horrors, denying them even a second of contentment their entire lives. They spend their lives jammed together, unable to move, breathing toxic air filled with ammonia from their droppings. More than 9 billion chickens a year are killed in the United States; worldwide 50 billion chickens or more are killed every year.

People mistakenly assume that free-range, organically fed poultry are humanely treated; however, unless the eggs and animals are purchased from small organic farms where one knows with certainty that the animals are treated well and allowed to live out their natural lives, the animals may well be abused.

Eat consciously. Reflect upon the chicks that don't completely break out of their shells: a machine will crash down on them, often causing dismemberment or death. Live male chicks of egg-laying hens are ground up in a giant blender or suffocated in a plastic bag.

Surviving chicks undergo debeaking without anesthesia, an experience traumatic enough to kill many of them. Survivors face more horrors. Each chicken is allowed a space the size of a page of copy paper or less (this is true of many free-range chickens as well), forced to become obese very quickly, and genetically controlled to grow immense breasts, perhaps dying from heart failure as a result. Should they survive, they must stand on legs not designed for huge breasts, causing them great pain. Egg-laying hens are starved during forced molts.

Fattened chickens are dumped onto a conveyor belt of death, hung upside down, their feet shackled. They go through a stunning tank, but so quickly they may still be conscious when their throats are cut, and the throat may not be cut. Dead or alive, they are dropped into boiling water to loosen feathers. Alive and conscious, countless chickens struggle to escape the scalding water. Gene Baur, who has devoted his life to helping factory farm animals, describes the poultry industry at length in *Farm Sanctuary*.

Every meal of chicken, turkey, eggs or foie gras (from ducks) finances cruelty. Choose actions that mirror back to you a kind, compassionate person, step away from participation in cruelty.

There are egg substitutes for baking and cooking; for instance, a tablespoon of ground flax seeds can be substituted for an egg in cookie recipes. Flax seeds have no cholesterol, and they provide omega-3, omega-6 and omega-9 fatty acids, protein, fiber, calcium and iron. Google "egg substitutes" to learn about other egg alternatives. There is no need whatsoever to eat poultry or eggs.

We are placing insurmountable obstacles in the way of wild birds. An estimated 12-25% of bird species are in danger of extinction in the coming decades, and countless more are at risk thereafter. North America has more than a billion less birds than 40 years ago, especially from grassland being converted to agriculture and from the use of pesticides and herbicides. Human activity in North America —vehicles (including airplanes), buildings, power lines, feral and domestic cats. urbanization, deforestation and farming —kills billions of birds yearly.

To save the birds, we must change. Despite irrefutable DNA evidence that *Homo sapiens* is an animal species related to all other animals, we persist in viewing ourselves as separate from and superior to nature, entitled to do as we wish. We are destroying the birds. May we wake up.

Toxicant/intensive agriculture kills birds. Earthworms and other organisms that compost dead and dying plant matter cannot thrive when chemical fertilizers are used, and so birds lose a food source. Pesticides kill the insects that insectivorous bird species consume. When rains wash the toxicants from intensive agriculture into ponds, lakes, rivers and the sea, algal blooms occur, resulting in dead zones that kill the food sources of waders, waterfowl and seabirds. Herbicides destroy wildflower seeds that seed-eating birds depend upon for survival. In addition, huge harvesters leave no grains for birds to eat, and they crush ground-nesting birds.

Hunting for food and sport is decimating birds, particularly migratory species such as ducks, geese and cranes, but also game birds like pheasants and quail. Around

5-10 billion passenger pigeons were killed in the the United States during the 19th century, until they became extinct in the wild by 1900. The Carolina parakeet disappeared, too, and it is believed hunting played a large role.

Lead bullets, lead shotgun pellets and lead pellets used to weight the fishing lines of anglers kill raptors, vultures, water birds and other birds. Birds swallow small pebbles to help their gizzard digest food, and they mistake lead pellets discarded by fishermen and hunters for stones. People from all over the world would gather to watch two critically endangered California condors at Big Bend in Zion. The condors died after eating the carcass of an animal a hunter had shot with a lead bullet. (Laws have been enacted in many European countries to prevent lead poisoning.)

Our society condones sport hunting. According to the dictionary, a sport involves exercise, skill, competition and entertainment. There are so many other ways to exercise, compete, become skilled, and find pleasure that there is no justification in killing for sport. Society is comprised of individuals. As individuals find killing for fun unacceptable, society will change. A shift in values is also urgently needed to save many parrot species and other caged birds. They become miserable when confined to a cage, and they are in peril of extinction.

Commercial fishing causes the deaths of untold numbers of birds. Factory ships take immense numbers of fish, and so seabirds go hungry/starve. The Atlantic puffin, for example, depends on sand eels to feed its young; it is willing to fly up to 60 miles every day to catch them. As commercial fishermen catch ever more sand eels, mostly for animal feed, puffin colonies disappear. In January, 2016, an estimated 8,000 dead murres washed up on Alaska beaches. They had starved to death, their food sources—small fish, crustaceans, squid and marine worms—gone; likely both climate change and fishing are to blame. Gill nets and longline fish hooks used in commercial fishing kill birds, too. Every year some 300,000 birds, including tens of thousands of endangered black-footed albatrosses, die when trying to eat the bait on the fish hooks.

There are immense numbers of deaths and extinctions connected with deforestation. Rain forests provide habitat for innumerable bird species, including parrots, eagles, hummingbirds, kingfishers and countless more. They die/ face extinction as tropical forests are destroyed (www.cowspiracy.com). Mangrove forests along tropical and subtropical coasts, the habitat for enormous numbers of birds, are being rapidly destroyed for development and shrimp farms. Deforestation causes more carbon to enter the sea, resulting in ocean acidification. Sea shells cannot form, coral reefs die, and birds lose more food sources.

We destroy birds as we replace salt marshes, coastal forests besides mangrove swamps, and other coastal habitats with development (vacation homes, resorts, farms, dumps, etc.), for many birds lose their habitat; migratory birds lose stopovers and wintering grounds. Effluent from factory farms and toxicant/intensive agriculture, industrial wastes, plastic, oil spills, drugs and other chemicals flow into rivers, lakes and the sea to kill birds.

Migratory birds are profoundly stressed by climate change. They time their journey to arrive at stopovers and breeding grounds when food sources are plentiful. Climate change disrupts this. Plants bloom earlier, or they are unable to adapt to climate change and disappear. Rivers and ponds dry up, threatening the birds that depend on them for survival. The decline in Antarctic krill, from sea ice melt, leads to starvation for chinstrap penguins and seabirds. Melting permafrost means the loss of a breeding ground for the red-breasted goose and numerous other species. Rising sea levels cause coastal habitats to disappear.

We are causing tremendous harm to birds with our food and lifestyle choices and human population growth. Eat consciously, live consciously. Let the birds sing, let them fly, let them be. Stop contributing to their destruction.

Each person can make a difference. During the 19th century, people killed all the puffins off the New England coast except one pair. In the 1960s, a teenage scientist, Stephen Kress, believed he could make a difference. He found ways to bring back the puffins, using decoys and some birds raised by hand; now there are hundreds of couples on islands off the Maine coast where he worked. He showed conservationists around the world ways to help seabirds.

## MAMMALS

250 million years ago some reptilian species began to change in ways that led to the class of mammals. Over time the jaw joint shifted. Jaw bones changed and relocated— ossicles in human ears were once part of the reptilian jaw joint. A secondary hard palate developed that let animals breathe and eat simultaneously. During the Triassic Period 245-208 million years ago, further changes occurred. Limbs were positioned under the body instead of at the side. The skull expanded to make room for a larger brain. Some species became endothermic.

The first mammals appeared around 225 million years ago. A mammal's brain averages 30 times larger than the brain of a comparably-sized reptile. The lower jaw of a mammal is formed from one bone, the dentary bone, rather than several bones. Mammalian teeth are specialized. They vary depending on diet, and they include incisors, canines, premolars and molars. The cheek teeth (molars and premolars) allow many mammalian species to crush plant food.

Mammals are endothermic, hence they must eat much more than ectothermic animals. Mammals have insulating hair or fur. Their hands typically have five fingers, though hoofed animals have lost one or more. Within these boundaries, there is fantastic diversity. Mammals have thrived since dinosaurs disappeared 65 million years ago. There are almost 5,500 living mammalian species, from tiny bats and mice to elephants and blue whales, inhabiting the land, rivers, lakes, sea and sky.

Mammals feed their babies with species-specific milk secreted by mammary glands. Milk guarantees the newborn(s) food. Suckling creates a powerful bond between a mother and her infant(s). I was fortunate to witness the tender moment a deer licked her newborn fawn clean then suckled it. The mother/infant bond is so strong that a mother reindeer will spend a week searching for her fawn if the fawn is lost during the migration to escape flies. Factory farm cows bellow inconsolably when robbed of their newborns; *The Telegraph* (March 30, 2009) reported that one cow escaped a farm and travelled 60 miles, probably in search of her calf. Factory farm sows often choose to stop eating when their piglets are taken from them, preferring death to life without their babies. A baby primate may die from grief should its mother be killed.

It is unnatural and unnecessary to consume the breast/teat milk of another species. It is no more natural or healthy to consume cow or goat teat milk in any form (cheese, butter, ice cream, yogurt, etc.) than to suckle from an elephant or whale or dog. Breast milk provides nutrition only for the young of a given species. Adults have different nutritional needs; breast milk is not intended for them.

Scientific research discussed by Campbell in *The China Study (CS)* links consumption of cow breast milk to breast, prostate and other cancers, osteoporosis, autoimmune disorders and more. Much animal protein is acidifying. To correct this the body takes calcium from bones as necessary. In countries where people don't drink cow breast milk, hip fractures among older women (an indicator of osteoporosis) are much less common than in countries where people consume dairy. Campbell writes more about the connection between dairy consumption and osteoporosis in *The China Study*, particularly regarding calcitriol, as well as inconsistencies in statistics of bone mineral density and bone health.

Too much calcium consumed consistently over time, as can happen with dairy consumption, creates an internal environment that leads to less production of 1,25 D, a form of vitamin D that fights many diseases and autoimmune disorders. Consumption of animal flesh can also block production (*CS*, 200). Cow breast milk contains a lot of fat, which the calf needs. However, high levels of saturated fat put a woman at risk of breast cancer. Dairy or other animal protein consumption can cause overproduction of the insulin-like growth factor IGF-1, linked to prostate cancer, as are diminished levels of 1,25 D (*CS*, 179-81). Furthermore, Campbell writes in *Whole* (written after *The China Study*) that "...casein is the most relevant chemical carcinogen ever identified" (*Whole*, 39). Casein is the primary protein in dairy products, and it is used in many processed foods, too.

Autoimmune disorders are linked to dairy consumption. For example, molecules of some cow breast milk proteins resemble molecules found in the human body. Should the milk proteins be only partially digested when they enter an infant's bloodstream, the body may form antibodies to attack them. These antibodies sometimes attack human cells that closely resemble the foreign proteins, perhaps leading to diabetes I, multiple sclerosis or other autoimmune diseases (*CS*, 186-92).

Cholesterol is found in dairy and all animal tissues, as well as saturated fat and dietary fat. When blood cholesterol accumulates on arterial walls as plaque, it decreases the flow of blood and hence the amount of oxygen delivered to cells, placing one at risk for heart attacks, strokes, Alzheimer's, cancers and more (*CS*, 106-07).

Dairy fat, as well as excess protein, can accumulate as layers of body fat, whereas the body burns excess carbohydrates from plant-based whole foods as body heat. People who eat a low fat vegan diet can consume more calories but weigh less than people who consume animal protein (*CS*, 142-43). The taste of fat tempts one, making it easy to spiral to obesity. There are healthy, cruelty-free comfort foods. Obesity is linked to diabetes II, which is associated with grave health problems such as the necessity for amputation of lower limbs, blindness, heart disease and more. Obesity makes exercise difficult, stresses the cardiovascular system and increases the likelihood of depression. Why risk suffering and ill health, why risk casting a deep shadow over your life that diminishes happiness?

Dairy purchases from factory farm animals support cruelty to cows and calves, goats and kids. Following public protest over the extreme abuse of veal calves, there have been some improvements in the ways the calves are treated, but some still endure wretched conditions (www.hfa.org), chained in small crates, unable to turn around or stretch their legs or lie down in a comfortable position, denied solid food, kept in darkness, deprived of drinking water. They experience chronic diarrhea and debilitating leg injuries because the crates have neither straw nor bedding. They never exercise, and they are forced to become obese very rapidly. They may be killed while conscious.

A dairy cow in a factory farm may spend her life on a stainless steel floor, unable to exercise, her teats cauterized and tails cut (both procedures performed without anesthesia). She is sprayed with pesticides and given hormones and antibiotics to produce a tremendous quantity of milk. When no longer productive, she is slaughtered, perhaps being dismembered while conscious, dying at some point; she may live up to seven minutes after her throat is slit.

The environmental costs are immense, including deforestation to grow animal food crops and up to 1,182 gallons of water for every gallon of cow breast milk ("River of Waste"). Deforestation causes countless more deaths and suffering to animals, while contributing to climate change, which brings about innumerable more deaths and extinctions.

Your next ice cream cone, yogurt, buttered toast, pizza, cookie or latte, see beyond the pleasure of taste. Remember the calves and the goat kids—their mothers' breast milk is meant for them, not you. Choose health for yourself and compassion for animals.

## RATS AND MICE AND MEN

During the time of the dinosaurs, mammals were the size of small rodents. Without their will and courage to survive, *Homo sapiens* might not have appeared. People tend to dislike rats and mice, but there are reasons to respect them. The mouse brain has 70 million neurons. A pinhead-size bit of brain contains a incredible amount of information—all brains, from those of rats and mice to human brains, are awesome.

Giant pouched rats in Africa were taught to help villagers after conflicts had left the land strewn with millions of land mines. Very intelligent, and having a keen sense of smell, they learned to detect the mines, and they weigh too little to set off any land mine accidentally. Villagers who had loathed the rats have come to appreciate them as good friends.

Much of what scientists have learned about rats is from lab research. Rats have self-awareness. They plan for the future, remembering where food is stored. Rats like to play tag, be tickled, wrestle with each other. They laugh/chirp, they bunny-hop for joy, they dread electric shock (*Animal Wise*, 116-31). Rats and mice teach us how mistaken our assumptions about other animals can be. They highlight how important it is to use substitutes to animal testing of cosmetics and household products, vivisection—any research that involves animal cruelty. The good news is that there has been a shift away from animal testing. For example, a UK firm is inventing alternatives that are superior to animal testing for chemicals in cosmetics and household products that include artificial models of human skin and eyes reconstructed from human cells donated by cosmetic surgery patients. Cruelty-free products are labeled on the packaging.

Animals small and large need our help in a way that often goes unnoticed. Every day a million animals are killed on roads in the United States. An inexpensive deer alert, available at auto parts stores, warns deer and other animals of danger by producing an ultrasonic whistle. Every car owner should buy one to put on his front fender. However, a deer alert only works at speeds greater than 35 mph. May an inventor design an inexpensive alert device that works at any speed, and may consumers insist that car manufacturers install it on every motor vehicle! Ideally, corridors and tunnels should exist in National Parks and everywhere wildlife is at risk from traffic—they've been proven to be effective. Climate change makes the need for corridors to protect migratory species essential.

# ELEPHANTS

After the extinction of the dinosaurs, some mammals grew to great size. Fossil ancestors to elephants existed 55-35 million years ago. There were tens of millions of elephants inhabiting the Earth until around 2,000 years ago; only 1% remain. In 1800 there were still some 26 million elephants, but now there are perhaps 400,000. 100,000 African elephants were killed in the last decade—people prefer ivory trinkets to elephants. An estimated 96-98 elephants are being killed every day; much of the money earned from selling their tusks funds violent conflicts.

Elephants and sperm whales have the largest brains of all animals. The temporal lobe, associated with language, sound and memory, is more convoluted in elephants than in humans. Elephants recognize themselves in a mirror. Their brains have Von Economo cells, associated with empathy (*Animal Wise,* 155-57). Elephants are able to identify a person's ethnicity, age and gender from the sound of the speaker's voice. An elephant associates the sound of another elephant with a mental picture of that elephant, even when the two have been separated for many years. Elephants remember hundreds of other elephants; when groups meet, they hug each other with their trunks, filling the air with sounds of happiness.

Elephants live in groups consisting of a matriarch, her daughters, sisters and their young; adolescent males form changing groups of their own. A female elephant comes into estrus for only 2-4 days every five years. Gestation lasts nearly two years. The infant nurses for up to four years and learns what to eat by taking food from its mother's mouth. The mother stays close enough to her child to be able to touch him with her trunk.

Young elephants love to tussle and romp and chase birds. Mature elephants like to have fun, too, walking in a goofy way, for example. Should there be danger, the group, facing outward, will encircle the young, and the matriarch will charge at the intruder (usually human) if necessary. She may be killed while protecting the young. When the matriarch is killed, her family is distressed for 15 years or more, and there are fewer births within the group.

Elephants will help an injured elephant in their group to stand up, then support her, or an elephant will give a sick elephant water. An elephant was seen feeding an elephant that had an injured trunk. Elephants share our best qualities; may we learn to cherish them.

An elephant's trunk is an elongated nose and upper lip, fused, with tens of thousands of muscles. The trunk is used in some ways similar to how we use our arms and hands. A mother and her child link trunks. Elephants affectionately greet each other with their trunks; trunks can also express romantic feelings. Elephants hold the bones of lost friends or family members with their trunks, seeming to grieve. The trunk sucks in water, to be transferred to the mouth. On hot days it becomes a hose, in high water, a snorkel. The trunk helps with eating by reaching high branches or digging roots. At the tip of the trunk are two sensitive, finger-like extensions (one in Asian elephants), which let the elephant crack a peanut shell or hold a stick to scratch himself. The trunk can lift objects weighing 350kg/770 lb. An elephant smells with his trunk, and the trunk amplifies sounds (*Princeton Encyclopedia of Mammals [PEM]*, 90).

Big ears fan out to cool the elephant. Tusks are modified incisor teeth that continue to grow throughout the elephant's life, reaching up to 3m/10'. Elephants use their tusks to tear the bark off trees and to dig up roots.

Elephants spend much of their day searching for food. The paths they make are used by other animals, including humans. The insects they stir up as they walk feed birds. Elephants disperse seeds, and their dung is a fertilizer. They dig water holes that are used by many animals. Their extinction would lead to numerous other extinctions.

African elephants are at great risk of extinction, from poaching and habitat loss. As the human population continues to grow, roads and towns disrupt the elephants' migratory routes, and more land is claimed for grazing cattle and growing crops. Asian elephants are poisoned, and the forests are set on fire to clear space for palm oil plantations. Palm oil is used in snack foods such as potato chips and baked goods, margarine, soaps, lotions, etc. There are alternatives to palm oil—poisoning elephants and deforestation are both unnecessary.

Agriculture, the discovery of how to make fertilizer from phosphate in rocks, better nutrition, vaccines and better medical care have allowed the human population to grow. There are expected to be more than 9 billion people by 2050. 30% of the Earth's land surface is used to graze livestock. Elephants, too, require a lot of space. Human population growth, along with an animal-based diet and poaching, has placed elephants and countless other species at risk of disappearing forever. We must change. Elephants live in countries where people have little money. To save them from extinction, affluent people everywhere need to step up. Money is needed for education: job training; understanding the annihilation underway, the interconnectedness of all life and the intrinsic worth of elephants; organic farming techniques and the benefits of an organic vegan diet; and human population growth. Money is needed for elephant reserves and for more patrol of poachers. Websites of several organizations dedicated to saving the elephants are listed in *Sources*.

Money now spent on large homes, expensive SUVs, RVs, etc., and material possessions could be redirected to help save the elephants and other wildlife. Buying products that don't use palm oil will help save the Asian elephants. The ivory trade will collapse as each person decides elephants are more important than ivory trinkets. When enough people adopt an organic vegan diet, the collective consciousness will shift, and people everywhere will follow. Grazing land can then be returned to wildlife. Reflect carefully about how many children you choose to bring into this world. What an empty world we leave the young as we decimate other species!

There is wonderful news recently regarding elephant conservation. Drones equipped with infrared cameras and GPS thermal imaging and are being effectively used to halt nocturnal  poaching. Artificial intelligence and game theory algorithms are being used to anticipate movements of poachers. China has a ban on ivory trading. *The Guardian*, a British journal, is publishing elephant updates in Chinese to help stop illegal trade. In Kenya, Dr. Paula Mkhumbu has launched a campaign, Hands Off Our Elephants, which includes education and awareness, as native Africans often aren't familiar with their wildlife. Tuskers (elephants whose tusks are so large that they touch the ground) are being collared to minimize problems with farmers and to protect the elephants. The Ringling Brothers Circus has stopped using elephants. PZP, a fertility control vaccine, is replacing the horrific practice of flying above elephants and shooting them.

## MANATEES AND DUGONGS

The elephants' gentle, peaceful sea cousins, manatees and dugongs, need our help, too. They spend their lives eating sea grass in coastal areas. A mother and her calf are close; the calf suckles for more than a year-and-a-half. Manatees and dugongs never show aggression. Unfortunately, people like the way they taste, and they have killed them in great numbers. Plastic and pollution kill them. Speed boats crash into them, wounding, killing them; there are almost a million pleasure boats in the Miami harbor alone.

Solutions to the crises of climate change and extinction require that one act on behalf of all life, transcending selfishness. There are kind ways to find pleasure and thrill, and there is no need to eat these peaceful animals, no need to toss plastic bags or any trash into the sea. The manatees, dugongs and all marine life teach us to treasure the sea.

# CARNIVORES

Modern felids date back 26 to 38 million years ago. Lions once roamed Africa, India, China, even parts of Europe, but in the past 10,000 years humans have killed around 14,000,000 lions. From 1960 to 2010 the lion population declined from 400,000-450,000 to 20,000-30,000. Other great cats—cheetahs, tigers, jaguars, etc.—are also threatened.

Cats are beautifully designed predators. Lions run 58kmph/36mph, cheetahs 95kmph/60mph. They prefer to hunt at night; a reflective layer in their eyes, the *tapetum lucidum,* enables them to see up to six times better than humans in the dark. Retractable claws come forward to grab/ hold prey. Strong jaw muscles clamp down on the animal, carnassials shear flesh and crush bones. Carnassials consist of the third upper premolars and first lower molars, functioning like scissors. The front part of the upper carnassials is designed to crush bones. Cats have protuberances on their tongues called papillae that rasp flesh from bones (*PEM,* 480-81).

Lions prefer to eat huge meals every few days. They eat ungulates (hoofed animals) and sometimes smaller mammals, birds and reptiles. Males may join together in hunting an elephant or giraffe.

A lion pride is made up of 3-10 related adult females, their young, and two or three non-related males. Males, related or not, form separate groups. A male will kill young lions in order to father a child with the mother. Males also sometimes kill each other in territorial disputes (*PEM*, 628-35).

Trophy hunters kill lions because they are magnificent, and leopards are killed for their beautiful skins. Poachers kill the big cats, as do farmers and ranchers; cattle owners will lace a carcass with poison, killing an entire pride. Grazing land, land to grow food for livestock, and human population growth leave no room for the big cats. Farms, ranches and communities block routes to new habitats.

We have turned the planet into a killing field. May we learn to share the Earth with the big cats, to treasure them rather than annihilate them. The documentary *The Last Lions* captures the lions' nobility and bravery and the monumental challenges that confront them. (One can learn more at Cause an Uproar.) Understanding the urgency of the situation will help awaken people's hearts to act on behalf of the great cats.

## CECIL, IN MEMORIAM

A lion named Cecil was killed by a trophy hunter recently. Cecil was lured off a reserve, maimed by an arrow, then shot to death 40 hours later. There are pictures of Cecil's killer, Walter Palmer, on the internet. Palmer is a scrubbed-faced dentist with perfect white teeth and a fixed smile. Photos show him proudly posing beside Cecil's corpse, smiling brightly beside an endangered rhinoceros he killed and beside many other magnificent animals he killed—killing large animals is his passion. There is no point to any of these killings other than to get a rush or perhaps to prove his virility. The rush soon passes, I've been told, so it becomes necessary to kill again and again and again. My father, a physician, was a trophy hunter, too. He placed the heads of the animals he killed on the piano room walls. Though he rarely looked at them, I did for hours a day, years and years, while practicing the piano. They were my friends, senselessly killed. They had wanted to live.

Would it please Palmer to shoot a domestic cat or dog? Would he feel satisfaction were he to shoot his pets (if he has pets) before sitting down to a pleasant lunch? Would he shoot a neighbor's pet? A horse, a lion in a zoo? I doubt it, and I doubt he would feel comfortable killing a human.

Photos of him give me the impression that he is a conformist. Possibly he attends church, and probably he is perceived by family and friends as a nice guy. His patients may think him amiable; he has been successful enough (unless the money was inherited) to spend great sums of money killing large animals for pleasure. It seems plausible he returns home after killing a lion and contentedly pets his dog, his conscience compartmentalized.

Social context helps in understanding Palmer's desire to kill splendid animals, some (all?) of them in danger of extinction. Trophy hunting reveals the complacent, cruel, repulsive nature of species arrogance, which is akin to racism. Speciesism thrives in societies that esteem power and dominance. Trophy hunting is condoned in our society —doctors and dentists and lawyers and businessmen kill wonderful animals with impunity. After Cecil's death, airlines declined to transport animal trophies and ivory tusks, indicating that our values are shifting.

Violence to animals is woven into our social fabric. Trophy hunting, sport fishing and commercial fishing are cruel to animals, in fact all hunting and fishing when one understands that there is no need to consume animal protein. Abuse of factory farm animals, bull fights, cock fights, dog fights, killing animals to wear them or for assumed medicinal properties, are inexcusable, as is animal testing of products. Everywhere, every day there are convivial mealtime conversations as families and friends consume animal flesh and dairy, unaware or unconcerned about factory farm animal cruelty. Species arrogance streams through our collective consciousness, conscience-free cruelty to animals is directly or indirectly part of our daily lives.

People objectify animals, denying the reality that they are sentient beings that don't deserve to be killed. Any moral distinction between killing an animal for pleasure and murder disappears the more aware one becomes of all that we share with lions and elephants and dolphins, cows and pigs and chickens and goats, cats and dogs, etc., from cells, tissues, organs and systems to intelligence and empathy. Understanding dissolves imaginary boundaries set to exclude nonhuman animals from ethical considerations.

Society is comprised of individuals. As each person comes to understand how wrong it is to kill animals for pleasure (trophy hunting, fashion), or because they are perceived as a threat to livestock, and how wrong it is to abuse factory farm animals, then society will cease to condone any animal cruelty. The belief that humans are more important than other animals has led to abuse and devastation. All life is miraculous. We make a tremendous mistake as we force our family of animals to extinction, and whenever we are cruel to them.

One rationale for hunting is that our ancestors were hunter-gatherers. However, we have deeper, vegetarian roots. Hunting as proof of power is a charade—an animal stands no chance against a gun. Hunting with a bow and arrow may present more challenges, but it is still unjustifiable. Whatever weapon the hunter uses, the animal is often left wounded.

Hunting is a more complicated matter for indigenous people in northern climates that depend on animals for food, and where growing produce is difficult. This doesn't alter the fact that humans have a vegetarian physiology. Though Inuits and other native people rely on animal flesh as a significant part of their diet, animal protein consumption nevertheless puts one at risk for numerous illnesses. People who eat an organic, low fat, whole foods vegan diet minimize the chance of fearsome diseases.

Vegan meals can be splendid. It is a pleasure to eat vegetables and fruits—the beautiful colors and shapes, the delicious tastes, especially after one stops eating fatty, sugary, salty foods. It is enjoyable to purchase organic produce at the local farmer's market. When one eats a whole foods vegan diet, exercise becomes fun, and one can effortlessly avoid weight gain.

Plants such as seeds, nuts, grains, beans, legumes and other vegetables provide protein. Organic produce and grains have all the nutrients one needs; only $B_{12}$ may need to be supplemented. The body requires only a small amount of $B_{12}$. It is present in the soil, but it is rinsed away when one washes vegetables. There is a common genetic mutation that prevents absorption of the most prevalent forms of $B_{12}$; a nutritionist recommended hydroxo $B_{12}$ to me.

People often form an allegiance to their diet. Many who eat animal flesh and dairy are fond of bacon and hamburgers and sweets. However, there are delicious vegan cookie and cake recipes, ice cream substitutes, and some veggie burgers taste fine. Beyond taste, there is no reason to eat bacon; the World Health Organization recently announced that processed meats are carcinogenic. There are excellent vegan cookbooks, and many recipes are available online at websites such as forksoverknives.com.

The carnivores we take into our homes and hearts—cats and dogs—teach us about love, loyalty and generosity. They teach us that nonhuman animals feel pain, suffer. Dogs are pack animals and prefer the company of other dogs, so it is good to adopt more than one dog if feasible. When adopting a cat or dog, be kind, choose a rescue pet; poppy mills subject especially the mother dogs to abuse. Dogs suffer when left alone outside or when chained, and they need to be protected from cars by fenced yards. However, for the most part, we do our best to treat our pets well; we need only extend that kindness to animals everywhere to rightfully view ourselves as a moral species.

Cats and dogs teach us another vital lesson. Globally, tens of millions of stray and feral cats and dogs are killed every year. In the United States, a shelter cat or dog may be euthanized every time one selects a pet from a breeder. Money is urgently needed to fund research for an inexpensive, easily administered female contraceptive, to establish no-kill shelters, and to educate people to spay/neuter and to adopt a shelter pet.

Our pets teach us to see past selfishness, to understand money as an active way to help animals in need, and to experience ourselves as belonging to a global community. How well we learn these lessons is up to us.

Our pets teach us about friendship between species. A recent newspaper story reported a blind man who fell onto a subway track; his seeing-eye dog lay by his side as the train passed over them (both survived). After 9/11 a golden retriever named Bear worked 18 hours a day for six months to find survivors and bodies among the wreckage. There were asbestos and other carcinogens at the site; perhaps this is the reason cancer spread throughout Bear's body, killing him a year after he had helped so much.

A dog, Matani, and a cheetah named Kosy became fast friends, as did a bear, Lucky, and a dog, Clika; a donkey, Whister, and a dog named Safi; a fox, Copper, and a hound named Jack. A grieving elephant, Terra Bella, found happiness when a dog befriended her. A cat and a crow became friends, as did a bear, lion and tiger. An orangutan named Tonda was despondent over the loss of her mate until a kitten became her playmate. She then felt so happy that she kept turning somersaults.

Animals other than carnivores also teach us about interspecies friendships. An elephant, Temba, moved past grief when a sheep sought out her friendship. Another sheep befriended a grieving white rhino calf, and a grieving black rhino, Omni, formed a close bond with a husky warthog named Digby. A baboon fostered a bush baby, a fox and a badger became friends. Animals accept interspecies friendships, as we do with our pets. We must befriend animals other than pets—they're our relatives, too.

## PINNIPEDS

Pinnipeds, including seals, walruses and sea lions, are marine members of the carnivore family that often live in cold climates. They have streamlined bodies. Their front limbs are modified as flippers, but they breed on land, and they can move more quickly over rocky terrain than humans. Pinnipeds have big eyes. Many have a combination of fur and blubber. The canines of male walruses grow into tusks, used as leverage on land and to establish dominance. Like elephants, walruses are killed for their tusks.

The pinniped's respiratory system is adapted to diving. Elephant seals sometimes dive down 1,500m/ 5,000'. They exhale before diving, and their lungs collapse when submerged. Their heart rate may slow down to two beats/minute. Myoglobin stores oxygen in their muscles. Blood to extremities and less essential organs is redirected to the heart and brain.

Lacking blubber, the sea otter has the densest fur of any animal. After diving to collect mussels, sea urchins and crabs to eat, a sea otter may lie on his back and use a stone to break open the shell placed on his stomach. A nap among giant kelp may follow. A baby otter likes to ride on top of its mother. The sea otter population has declined more than 90% in recent years, from hunting and toxic wastes polluting the sea.

For a brief time young harp seals have a fur coat that people desire. Every year hunters in Greenland and Canada, with government support, shoot or club 2- or 3-weeks-old baby seals to death. 100,000 are killed in Greenland every summer, and nearly that number are killed in Canada. In addition, there are 100,000 killed but not included in the official count, plus older seals left wounded to die (*PEM*, 568-69). There is no need to wear fur; synthetic materials provide as much warmth. Many people in these countries eat seal meat; alternatives must be found that don't involve hammering infant seals to death. Demand for the pelts of the young seals has decreased, and some major fashion designers now refuse to use fur. Public protest has made a difference, but there is much more to do.

## HOOFED ANIMALS

Most large animals are hoofed, with long, slender legs designed for running. They run on tiptoe. Some run very fast indeed—the pronghorn can run 86kmph/53mph. Nearly all hoofed animals (ungulates) are herbivorous, with teeth that can grind grains and other plant foods. Ungulates ferment food. This occurs in the cecum and colon in horses and zebras. There is a four-chambered stomach in ruminants such as deer and giraffes and cows. Fermentation occurs in the rumen, then it is regurgitated, chewed again, and passed through three other stomach chambers, with more fermentation in the cecum. Digestion takes more than three days (*PEM*, 676-79).

Around 65 million years ago, ungulates separated into perissodactyls (odd-toed) and artiodactyls (even-toed). Artiodactyls include deer, antelopes, cattle and other bovids, camels and their relatives, giraffes, pigs, peccaries and hippopotamuses. Horses, zebras, asses, tapirs and rhinoceroses are the surviving perissodactyls. Ungulates are threatened by human activity. For example, tapirs, piglike animals found in Central and South America, are killed for food, trophies and folk medicine remedies, and many are captured for zoos. Humans have brought them disease and caused inbreeding, while destroying their habitat (*PEM*, 696-97). Tapirs are major seed dispersers for palm, avocado, and other trees, as well as for bromeliads and ferns, and their feces fertilizes and mulches—they are essential to their forest ecosystem.

## GIRAFFES

Giraffes are the tallest animals, with remarkably long, slender necks and legs; they reach up to 5m/16'. Giraffes eat foliage, shoots, fruits and flowers. A long tongue (46cm/18") and flexible lips help the giraffe to reach food. Molars crush plant shoots, and a gap between molars and canines lets the giraffe strip leaves from twigs. Giraffes are ruminants like deer and cattle; food travels back up their neck to be chewed again. The giraffe's neck has seven vertebrae, the same as other mammals. Carotid arteries branch out into a network of small blood vessels at the base of the brain to keep the brain from bursting when the giraffe bends over to drink. Thick, tight skin around the lower legs prevents blood from spilling out of blood vessels.

The patterns and coloring of a giraffe's coat, unique to each animal, provide camouflage in the savanna woodlands. The plants giraffes eat are seasonal, so they must travel over a wide range in search of food. They travel in groups of twenty or less. Males use their necks and heads to wrestle and butt each other during the mating season. A mother gives birth to a single calf after a 15-month gestation, then nurses her baby for up to 18 months. She will kick predators to protect her calf (*PEM*, 742-48).

Giraffes need space, space that is disappearing as people take over land to graze cattle. Cattle owners on communal grazing lands kill the giraffes whenever they wish, leaving the flesh to rot. Education about organic vegan farming methods and the health benefits of an organic vegan diet, alongside the risks linked to animal protein consumption, is key to saving giraffes from pointless slaughter.

## MIGRATORY HERDS

Many hoofed animals migrate in huge numbers to find food, water and minerals, and to escape flies or predators: reindeer and caribou and pronghorn antelopes in northern locations; gazelles in Mongolia; tiang and other antelopes in the Sahel; wildebeest, zebras and Thomson's gazelles in Tanzania.

Every year as the dry season approaches, up to 1.5 million wildebeest, 250,000 zebras and 300,000 gazelles migrate from the short-grass plains southeast of Serengeti

National Park, northwest along the wetter edges of Lake Victoria, to the Masai Mara Preserve, where they stay during the dry season, returning to the short-grass plains as the rains begin again. They migrate to where there is sufficient phosphorus in the soil, without which they have problems with fertility, milk production, bones, teeth and growth— sometimes a phosphorus deficiency even causes death. They also migrate to find food and water and to escape predators. Many lose their lives at river crossings during the migration, ambushed by crocodiles. They depend on the Mara River for water, but the amount of water in the river is increasingly unpredictable.

Settlements, ranches, farms, fences and roads create obstacles along migratory routes. There is ever increasing competition for water and food as the human population grows and more land and water are claimed for livestock.

## CATTLE

The domestication of cattle, descended from aurochs, started around 10,000 years ago. People began to kill wildlife in order to claim the land for grazing cattle. There was frenzied killing in the United States during the 19th century, when 90 million bison were shot to death. European bison disappeared in the early 19th century. The United States Wildlife Services killed 4 million animals in 2013 and 2.7 million in 2014 (Wiki/*Wildlife Services*); the animals are shot, poisoned, or set on fire. Conservation groups such as Defenders of Wildlife say that the killing is conducted on behalf of the livestock industry and has led to the near-extinction of dozens of species. South American rain forests are burned to create grazing land (www.cowspiracy.com); billions of fast food hamburgers eaten in the United States are from South American cattle. Tamarins, parrots, sloths, snakes and innumerable other species are destroyed. The soil quickly turns to hard dirt, leading to erosion. Droughts occur more often, triggering forest fires that kill more wildlife.

Livestock excrement poisons rivers and the sea, causing algal blooms that result in die-offs of great numbers of fish, amphibians, etc. Methane produced by cattle and other farm animals is a far more potent greenhouse gas than carbon dioxide, as is nitrous oxide, which results from waste handling of livestock excrement. Simple organic ways to create a healthy soil, described in the chapter on plants, insects and earthworms, are a better option.

Cattle consume great quantities of water—70% of the water in the western United States. The immense Ogallala

Aquifer is being rapidly depleted, in large part because of cattle (circleofblue.org/Water News) Cattle eat five times as much grain as do people in the US. Sixteen pounds of corn are needed to produce a pound of beef.

Free-range animals aren't a viable alternative. They cause desertification by trampling the land. They produce methane. They use corn and soy from abroad for animal feed, contributing to deforestation and to fuel consumption during transportation. They pollute streams and consume much water. They suffer an awful fate at the slaughterhouse. Despite the large federal deficit, cattlemen in the western United States pay little for grazing cattle on public lands. It is important to elect legislators that refuse to support subsidies to the livestock industry and intensive agriculture.

Cattle are abused. A calf may be auctioned soon after birth, denied its mother's affection and nourishment, leaving the mother bereft. Cattle are drugged with antibiotics, given hormones, sprayed with pesticides. During transport, cattle are crammed together, some crushed to death, others injured. The injured cows, 'downers', are dragged with chains or ropes, or scooped up with tractor shovels. Cattle may be transported in extreme heat or cold, without water or food, forced to stand/lie on their excrement. Electric prods are jammed into their faces or rectums should they be slow to move off the 18-wheeler (peta.org). They may be skinned and dismembered while conscious and it may take many minutes for one to die after his throat is slit.

Public outcry makes a difference; for example, the California Downed Animal Law forbids any farm, stockyard or auction to buy, sell, receive or transport downers—non-ambulatory animals (cows, pigs, goats and sheep)—for sale commercially for humans to consume (hfa.org). Responding to people's concern for animals, Walmart states that it is committed to the 5 freedoms for farm animals—freedom from hunger, discomfort, pain, distress, and freedom to express normal behavior—but the only way to really accomplish this is to become vegan, as the desire to maximize profits is likely to override kindness to factory farm animals. Laws such as the Humane Slaughter Act protect some farm animals, though poultry are excluded. Millions of dollars are allocated yearly to ensure enforcement, but the animals may not truly be protected, as slaughter houses may adjust their behavior when an inspector is present. Many states, including Utah, have ag-gag laws that make it illegal to photograph or record the anguished sounds of factory farm animals, and for animal rights advocates to seek employment on factory farms under false pretenses. Fines range from $1,000 to $50,000 and/or

1-10 years in prison! There are also state constitutional amendments meant to silence people concerned with farm animal welfare.

Eating hamburgers supports abuse. People accept cruelty to farm animals that they would never allow to happen to their pets. The abuse occurs out of sight, thus some may be unaware of it, though documentation is readily available online. Misguided beliefs that one needs animal protein and that humans are omnivores are factors, but the abuse of cattle and all factory farm animals may reflect, too, a belief in human superiority—that we are entitled to treat other animals as we wish. Speciesism, passed on from generation to generation, can lead otherwise well-meaning, kindhearted people to participate in animal cruelty with their food choices. The good news is that scientists are making in vitro meat from minute samples of living animals, and they are inventing plant-based foods that mimic the texture and taste of animal flesh for those who love the taste of a hamburger. Also, synthetic leathers are improving in quality.

Campbell found that increased animal protein consumption beyond 10% of one's diet furthers liver cancer development at every stage. Regardless of the amount of plant protein consumed, this never happened (*CS*, 66). A

*Washington Post* article March 4, 2014, entitled "Too much protein could lead to early death, study says", reports the findings of U.S. and Italian researchers that studied hundreds of adults for two decades. Those that ate a high (mostly animal) protein diet (20%+) when middle-aged were four times more likely to develop cancer than people who ate a low protein diet (10% or less)—a high protein diet proves to be as risky as smoking.

A hamburger tells a story of cruelty, countless deaths, deforestation, desertification, climate change and extinctions. We are not the only species whose young want to play. We are not the only animals that want to live, who yearn to touch and be touched, we are not the only species to suffer. Choose kindness, see beyond taste.

## PIGS

Baur describes a lovely friendship between two pigs at one of his sanctuaries. Hope, an older rescue pig, was weak. Other pigs would steal her food until Johnny, a younger rescue pig, was brought to the sanctuary. He looked out for Hope, guarding her while she ate. They slept side by side and spent their days together. (*Farm Sanctuary,* 128-29).

Pigs are subjected to as much or more abuse than any other factory farm animals. I wish every American would watch *Death on a Factory Farm*, a documentary of animal cruelty on a hog farm. An undercover investigator for the Humane Farming Association (HFA), "Pete", filmed baby pigs being torn from their mothers, thrown into a pen, then tossed again onto a school bus to fatten. The mothers would often die from grief. Undersized piglets were held by their back legs, their heads smashed against the concrete floor or bashed with a hammer. Injured, sick sows were hanged to death with a chain attached to a front loader. It took 4-5 minutes to die, minutes of terror, minutes of extreme pain. In a subsequent trial, the ways the piglets and sows were killed were deemed acceptable forms of euthanasia, though euthanasia is defined as a pain-free, compassionate death for the terminally ill.

Millions of factory farm pigs are forced to live in the worst imaginable conditions. Sows are immobilized in small metal crates without bedding during a four-month gestation. (Though many companies claim that they are phasing out these terrible crates, often they either set a date many years from now, or none at all. Legally, they can claim to not use one even when the sows are kept in crates for two months, until the embryo is proven to be viable.) Their feces accumulates, making the air toxic. They are given no exercise, no affection; the extreme distress leads them to repetitively rub their snouts across the crate or bite the metal bars. The sows give birth, nurse, eat, sleep, defecate, drink in a crate. Some states and corporations have banned gestational crates, but this doesn't guarantee that the pigs will be treated well. The sows may be impregnated immediately after birth. Their piglets are stolen from them while still dependent upon them. At the end of their unhappy lives they are slaughtered; like cattle, they may be conscious when skinned and dismembered, taking minutes to die. Help end the brutality, stop eating bacon or any pig flesh.

## CETACEANS

Cetaceans (whales, dolphins and porpoises) are most closely related to hippopotamuses, then to deer and antelopes. Fossil evidence of cetaceans dates back millions of years. Cetaceans have a streamlined, hairless body and a horizontal tail fin. They traverse the sea with up/down movements of their tail flukes. They breathe air through a blowhole on the top of their head. Cetaceans nurse their young with milk. They are endothermic like other mammals.

Cetaceans have some of the largest brains of all animals. Their brains may have three times as many spindle cells as humans; these are associated with communication and emotions. Emotional awareness and empathy have been observed in gray whales off the coast of Mexico, for example. Some cetaceans have been seen to protect a wounded member of their group, and a mother grieves if her child dies. Cetaceans are divided into two groups, toothed whales and baleen whales. Toothed whales rely on echolocation to communicate and to find prey. Toothed whales eat fish, squid, and sometimes seabirds and other marine mammals, while baleen whales filter plankton and small fish.

## SPERM WHALES

Sperm whales, reaching up to 20m/65', are the biggest toothed whales, and they may have the largest brain of any animal that ever existed; the forehead of the sperm whale occupies up to a quarter or more of his body. A sperm whale will dive deeper than 3,000m/9,800' to catch giant squid. Thick skin and blubber keep him warm. He can hold his breath for an hour. His ribs bend to withstand 2,000 pounds of pressure. He eats up to a ton of food a day, digested in a three-chambered stomach and intestines. Sperm whales sometimes mate belly-to-belly like humans. The calf suckles up to 13 years. Sperm whales travel in groups. Clans have unique dialects, ways of hunting and which prey is selected —they have culture. When one is injured, the others encircle him. This has made it easy for whalers to harpoon them.

Spermaceti is a white waxy substance located in a rounded organ in the sperm whale's head that focuses acoustic signals and aids in buoyancy. "Monkey lips" attached to the spermaceti smack to produce clicks. Air pops out of the lips and travels through the spermaceti, then out a tiny hole in the whale's right nostril. The returning echoes give the whale a sonar picture to locate prey. Sperm whales produce the loudest sounds of all animals, which can be heard up to 40 miles away. Sperm whales are affected by noise pollution from sonar testing. They become disoriented, can't find prey, starve. In addition, commercial fishermen increasingly fish the deep sea, leaving them little food.

Some 750,000 sperm whales have been killed since 1712 for their spermaceti, for chemical products, and to be used as pet food. For half a century, until the whaling ban went into effect in the mid-1980s, 20,000 sperm whales were killed yearly; 46,000 whales were killed in 1937-1938.

Explosive harpoons used after World War II decimated them; only around 350,000 remain. Despite the ban on commercial whaling, Iceland, Japan, Russia, Norway, Greenland and Canada continue to kill whales (*PEM*, 811).

## DOLPHINS AND PORPOISES

Dolphins are small toothed whales, with beaks and curved dorsal fins. We delight in their playfulness, intelligence, beauty and joy. The last common ancestor dolphins shared with primates was 95 million years ago, and their last common ancestor with other mammals was 55 million years go.

Dolphins are social animals that form longterm bonds. They seem to have language and perhaps even syntax, and they identify themselves with specific click patterns. Dolphins are curious. They have self-awareness, recognizing themselves in mirrors. Each spotted dolphin has a unique whistle similar to a name. They are affectionate with each other and often with humans, swimming alongside boats; even orcas (large killer whale dolphins) sometimes befriend humans. Dolphins will help a person or animal in distress. Off the Ireland coast, a dolphin named Duggie became close friends with a golden retriever called Ben. They would play together hours at a time, and should Ben tire, Duggie would support him and guide him back to shore.

Dolphins body-surf breaking waves, seeming to leap out of the air just for fun sometimes. In one experiment, when researchers made bubble rings, dolphins played with the rings for hours. After eating, dolphins like to have sex, touch each other and swim belly to belly. When reconnecting after a lengthy absence, spinner dolphins will make lots of clicks, spin in the air and touch each other. Dolphin males form pairs and trios to court then control females. The bond between males can last decades. Males also form larger groups of 4-14; the gangs fight over females. Dolphin alliances are complicated, one likely reason for their large brain. They have friends and enemies, and relationships can change frequently.

Porpoises and dolphins shared a common ancestor 10 million years ago. Porpoises are smaller than dolphins and lack a rostrum (beak-like projection). They have a small triangular dorsal fin and spade-shaped teeth (rather than the conical teeth of dolphins).

Echolocation is vital to survival for dolphins and porpoises. Sounds are produced in a nasal sac region inside the blowhole. They make clicks, mostly ultrasonic (above the audible range of humans), up to 600/second. These are focused by a fat-filled, lens-shaped melon on the forehead. Returning echoes from objects travel through oil-filled sinuses in the lower jaw to the inner ear, giving the dolphin a detailed sound picture of his surroundings (*PEM*, 802-04). Sonar from military and ships interferes with echolocation. The dolphins become disoriented and depressed, and some die after being stranded on a beach. However, NOAA (National Oceanic and Atmospheric Administration) is drafting plans to reduce noise pollution by 2026. The public is encouraged to offer comments to help improve the plans at comments.ONS@noaa.gov. Ocean acidification may also adversely affect echolocation. In addition, thousands of dolphins and porpoises are caught in fishing nets every year, to be discarded dead or dying as by-catch. Collisions with ships kill many dolphins and porpoises, and toxins and trash (especially plastic bags) kill large numbers—we use the sea as a gigantic trash bin.

## BALEEN WHALES

Baleen whales eat by sifting plankton and small fish from seawater with keratinous strips of whalebone hanging from their upper jaw. One baleen whale species, the blue whale, is the largest mammal ever to live on Earth, reaching up to 27.4m/90'. Some live for centuries. Blue whales go on some of the longest migrations of any mammals, swimming at speeds of up to 48.3kmph/30mph. They are affectionate, using their fins to hug each other. Blue whales feed on krill. They dive hundreds of feet beneath the krill, then swim up through huge numbers of them, straining them with baleen. The population of blue whales has declined from 300,000 before whaling began to less than 10,000 now. Though there is a ban on whaling, blue whales and other baleen whales are threatened by krill depletion and collisions with ships; shipping traffic has killed an estimated 98% of the blue whale population.

Another baleen whale species, the humpback whale, is famous for the songs the males sing during mating season. Humpbacks grow up to 15m/50' long. They like to breach (rise and break through the water surface). Humpback courtship is intense. After the female fin slaps to indicate she is ready to mate, males go with her on a long swim. They are aggressive towards each other until the female selects her mate, then they make peace by caressing one another. Humpback friendships endure. They form groups to hunt herrings. After they all dive together and move into position, herders encircle the herrings. A caller emits a scream to force the fish to rise, then the ring leader blows a net of bubbles to trap them. Finally, the group swims up through the shoal with open mouths to feast.

The gray whale, a baleen whale, will stand erect with part of his body out of water (spy-hopping). His spout reaches up to 3m/10'. During dives, gray whales may remain underwater for one-and-a-half hours. Gray whales migrate from the Bering Sea near the Arctic Ocean to Baja California in Mexico, a roundtrip of 20,000km/12,400mi. They were hunted until their numbers dropped to a few hundred, but conservation efforts have succeeded in bringing their population back to around 25,000. Gray whales appear to feel empathy. In 1972, a gray whale off the Mexican coast swam beside a fisherman's boat to be stroked, seemingly as forgiveness for the way whalers in that region had decimated them prior to the whaling ban. They are remarkably friendly to humans, giving tourists great pleasure as they swim alongside boats.

Right whales are so named because they trust humans and hence were the right whale to kill. Some weigh 80 tons and have a 9-foot penis, but they are gentle lovers. The bowhead whale, or Arctic right whale, is three times as big as the gray whale. To survive year-round in the Arctic Sea, it keeps warm with a two-foot layer of blubber weighing up to

50 tons. Analysis of amino acids from one bowhead proved it to be 200 years old. Northern white whales were some of the first whales to be hunted commercially. They are critically endangered, with a population of only 300-350. They were killed for trivial uses such as corsets and umbrellas.

## PRIMATES

Tropical forests are home to our fellow primates. Gibbons in Southeast Asia use their long arms to brachiate among the trees. Orangutans dwell in the forests of Borneo and Sumatra. New World monkeys can be found in Central and South America, Africa is home to chimpanzees, bonobos, gorillas, Old World monkeys and other primates.

The first true primates appeared 60 million years ago. Extant species range from lemurs that weigh around an ounce to 385-pound gorillas. Primates have forward-facing eyes; stereoscopic vision allows them to judge distances when moving among the trees. Many species have opposable thumbs or toes that help them to grasp branches. Nearly all primates have nails rather than claws. Though fur or hair covers their bodies, the face is often naked, making facial expressions clear.

The majority of primates are primarily vegetarian; more than half of the species eat mostly fruit. Many species have trichromatic vision that helps them discern differences among greens, reds, yellows and oranges, in order to know which fruits are ripe. In addition to fruits, primates eat shoots, leaves, insects, worms and frogs. Chimpanzees and bonobos occasionally eat larger mammals like monkeys and duikers; however, they may go months without eating such an animal.

Primate society centers around the mothers and children. Primate brains are proportionally three times bigger than those of other mammals. Primates tend to have long lifespans, with an extended youth period for learning, which necessitates a larger brain. The neocortex, linked to creative thinking, sight and sounds, has thickened in primates, especially humans (*PEM*, 281).

Prosimians ("before apes"), also called strepsirrhines ("wet noses"), are primates that most closely resemble early primates. They include the lorises of South India, Southeast Asia, Malaysia and Indonesia; bush babies and pottos of Africa, India and Southeast Asia; and the lemurs of Madagascar. The three groups diverged around 40 million years ago. Prosimians have longer snouts than most other primates. The bush babies, lorises and pottos are small nocturnal primates. Bush babies, only 10.5-47cm/4-18.5″, can leap across 20-foot spaces in the forest canopy. The forests of Madagascar, off the African coast, have 35 different lemur species, whose ancestors probably rafted to the island on vegetation tens of millions of years ago. There are sifakas, standing erect, maybe with babies on their backs, arms and tail stretched out for balance, that bound exuberantly on the ground; ring-tailed lemurs, their long tails held straight up; the aye-aye (allied to lemurs), with an incredibly long, thin middle finger for reaching grubs in tree bark. Gorilla-sized lemurs were hunted to extinction when humans settled Madagascar around 2,000 years ago.

New World monkeys, the only primates in the Western hemisphere, probably traveled to the Americas on vegetation rafts from Africa. The earliest fossils date back 27 million years. They are classified as platyrrhines ("flat noses"). Most larger species have a prehensile tail. Except for capuchins, New World monkeys lack an opposable thumb. Platyrrhines are found in the forests of Central America and South America. They live in treetops and eat fruits, nuts, seeds, leaves, tree gum, nectar, insects, invertebrates, frogs, lizards, and occasionally small mammals. There are 41 species, including tamarins, squirrel monkeys, capuchins, night monkeys, titis, spider monkeys and howler monkeys.

Capuchins use rocks as tools to smash nuts or retrieve honey. The tufted capuchins living in an arid region of Brazil have learned to use their tails to soak up water in holes, which they then lick. Titi couples spend their day holding hands, entwining tails, grooming each other, hugging, cuddling, kissing; they become very upset when separated from each other. Spider monkeys hang from their long tails while eating, using the tail as an extra limb.

Old World monkeys evolved around 15 million years ago. They are catarrhines, with narrow noses and downward-facing nostrils. No Old World monkey species has a prehensile tail. Old World monkeys have hardened skin called callosities on their bottoms. They are fruit-eaters. Old World monkeys include macaques, baboons, patas monkeys, mandrills and drills, colobus, proboscis monkeys, etc. Some Japanese macaques (or snow monkeys) endure the snowy winters by spending much of the day in a hot spring. Macaques are often used in research. When given a limited amount of food, they choose to share it rather than eat it all themselves. The patas monkey is the fastest primate, able to run 55kmph/35mph. Male mandrills, the largest of all monkeys, have amazing blue and red coloring on their faces.

The critically endangered Yunan snub-nosed monkeys live high in the Himalayas, up 4,200m/14,000′. They express gentleness and generosity, as well as aggression, in their interaction. Filmmakers for the documentary *Mystery Monkeys of Shangri-La* observed a father and other males help care for an infant rejected by its mother. This infant and his half-brother would play hide-and-seek together, do gymnastics, hug each other like best friends. Females act as midwives when another female gives birth. When one baby died, its mother carried the body for three days.

The ape family includes gibbons (lesser apes) and orangutans, gorillas, chimpanzees, bonobos and humans (great apes). Ape species generally are medium to large size, with no tail. They are barrel-chested, their shoulders and wrists are mobile, and they have long arms. They have opposable thumbs, forward-facing eyes and trichromatic vision. Their cheek teeth are designed to chew plant food. They remember where fruit trees are located and when the fruit is ripe. Excepting orangutans, apes form social groups. All (including orangutans) have faces that express many emotions. A large brain has helped apes to learn and to make tools.

18 million years ago gibbons diverged from the greater apes. The smallest, most slender apes, they live in forests of

Bangladesh, Borneo, Vietnam and China. Their long arms and fingers, with short thumbs, let them move with ease through the trees. Gibbons can jump up to 12m/40'. They form monogamous pairs that sing beautiful duets. The couple have one child every 2 to 4 years. Gibbons sleep sitting on branches. They eat mainly fruit, preferring figs. As seed dispersers, they are essential to the Southeast Asian forests, but gibbons are among the most endangered species on Earth.

Orangutans ("people of the forest"), that inhabit the forests of Borneo and northern Sumatra, are the largest tree-dwelling animals. They branched off from the other great apes 14 million years ago. Orangutans have shaggy orange fur and blue-grey skin. Males reach up to 141cm/55.5"; they weigh twice as much as females and far more than gibbons. An orangutan uses his legs as well as arms to move from tree to tree, swaying a branch back and forth until it is close enough to an adjacent tree for him to jump.

Orangutans spend much of their time alone. Most of their diet is fruit. All orangutans use leaves as umbrellas, and some make stick tools to obtain honey and termites. They sleep in the trees, every day building a new sleeping platform from leaves and sticks. An orangutan gives birth once every 8 or 9 years. The baby drinks only its mother's milk for 11 months, continuing to suckle for 5-6 years. Childhood lasts a long time, for the youngster must learn which plants to eat and which are poisonous, when fruit is ripe, which branches are strong enough to carry his weight, which insect nests to raid. Orangutans are very intelligent. They have culture, shown in the different building techniques groups use to make sleeping platforms, different vocalizations, and different ways of handling food.

Orangutans are in imminent danger of extinction from deforestation. 93% of the orangutan population was killed last century, and the remaining Sumatran population declined by half from 1993 to 2000. Young orangutans are also stolen for the pet trade (*PEM*, 400-403).

Gorillas, the largest primates, share 97% of their DNA with humans, more than they do with orangutans. They live in Central Africa, near the Congo Basin, from sea level to 12,400'. Gorillas are more terrestrial than arboreal, though the females and young often sleep in trees. In addition to fruit, gorillas eat leaves, saplings, bark, seeds and flowers; they devote much of the day to eating.

Gorillas knuckle walk on all four limbs. They have long arms and large hands. Males grow silver hair on their back during puberty. A silverback protects a harem of 5-15 females and their offspring. His large canines are to frighten competitors and predators. Otherwise, despite his huge size (averaging 156cm/61.5", 175kg/385lb.), a silverback spends his days eating, napping and playing with the young gorillas.

As the human population in Africa grows, people take over gorilla habitat to raise livestock and grow crops. Four of the six great ape species, all gorillas and orangutans, are critically endangered. Gorillas may become extinct within 150 years unless people everywhere help them (*PEM*, 392-96). An international treaty, the Agreement on the Conservation of Gorillas and Their Habitat, now exists.

The apes most closely related to humans, sharing around 99% of our DNA, are chimpanzees and bonobos. They are closer to us genetically than they are to gorillas. They live in the Congo River Basin, chimps on one side of the river, bonobos on the other. Chimps and bonobos are smaller than humans, with longer arms than legs, long fingers and mobile shoulder joints—adaptations for moving among the tree tops, where they eat and sleep. Though they can stand up, they prefer to knuckle-walk like gorillas, as their skeleton lacks adaptations for a bipedal posture. Fruit is their favorite food, with some leaves, flowers, seeds and other parts of plants, and termites. Chimps hunt monkeys and bonobos hunt antelopes, but only 5% or less of their eating time is spent consuming animal flesh. They have larger jaws and canines than humans, better suited for hunting and eating animals.

Chimpanzees and bonobos live in groups of 15-150 members; males dominate in chimp society and females in bonobo society. They have large brains and make tools such as twig probes, hammer stones and anvils, leaves used as sponges and napkins, and branches used as spears. They can solve problems and have discovered the medicinal value of some plants. They are able to recognize themselves in a mirror. Chimps have been studied in research labs a great deal, where they have learned sign language to symbolize objects, actions, even abstract concepts. Their brains are capable of language, but they lack the vocal apparatus to speak. They have been taught to use a computer to communicate, pressing different buttons for different words. They seem to understand that others, too, have thoughts and feelings. Chimpanzees and gorillas have eidetic memories— they remember in remarkable photographic detail.

Conflicts between groups of male chimpanzees from different groups sometimes result in death; they are the only mammals besides humans to kill this way. However, the fights are often followed by hand-shakes, lip smacking, and sometimes embraces and grooming. Chimps can also be generous, sharing a tool, for instance (*PEM*, 384-91).

Chimps and bonobos took separate paths 1.7-2.7 million years ago. Bonobos are more slender than chimps, have red lips, and their hair parts down the center of the top of the head. Males are much bigger than females. Bonobos are less aggressive than chimps; sex is their favorite way to reduce tensions between each other.

The chimp population declined from 2 million to 200,000 last century. They are at risk of extinction from logging, deforestation to clear land for livestock and crops, hunting for bushmeat, the pet trade, and capture for zoos and research labs. However, in June, 2015, endangered status was granted to lab chimps. ending to most invasive procedures. The National Institute of Health [NIH] subsequently stopped funding research that involved chimps. Lab chimps have been relocated to sanctuaries.

The human population in the Congo Basin doubled from the 1920s to 2005. As more roads are built, bushmeat hunters can easily shoot/snare chimps, bonobos, other primates, mammals, birds and reptiles. City people like to eat bushmeat, familiar to them from their rural childhood. Hundreds of millions of primates and other wildlife are killed yearly in the Congo Basin for the rural population alone; add to that the popularity of bushmeat in cities, and it becomes obvious why our fellow primates are likely to go extinct. Continued human population growth will worsen this tragic situation.

A young chimpanzee or orangutan stolen for the pet trade, research and zoos, suffers tremendously. He likely saw his mother being killed. Many young chimps and orangutans do not survive in captivity, and those that do are often abused.

Trees transpire, helping to bring rains. They use carbon dioxide in photosynthesis. Carbon is stored in tree bark, in the soil beneath trees, and in peat swamps; great amounts of carbon are released when the trees are destroyed. The forests need primates to disperse seeds. Without them and other seed dispersers, the forests are likely to go extinct. Primate conservation organizations are listed in *Sources* at the back of this book.

Plywood, cardboard and other paper products from forests of Southeast Asia are often not recycled. People purchase paper products not made from recycled paper because of the lower price, without consideration of the real costs described above. Big homes use more timber, which may come from Africa or Southeast Asia. When shopping, eating, or building a home, make choices that help to save the primates.

# HOMO SAPIENS

*Homo sapiens* is Latin for "wise man". We have language, music, art. We are capable of abstract thought, we are conscious that other people have thoughts and feelings, and we have awareness of right and wrong. What our bodies can do, from sports to dance, is awesome. We have built cities and civilizations. No wonder we view ourselves as superior to other animals! Yet we are discovering that we share more with them than we ever imagined.

Chimpanzees and hominids diverged 5 to 7 million years ago. 4 million years ago, our fossil ancestors began to live on the ground rather than in trees. Over the next 2 million years there were skeletal adaptations to a bipedal lifestyle. 2.6 million years ago stone tools were invented, and 2 million years ago the *Homo* genus appeared as the species *Homo erectus* (or *Homo ergaster*).

*Homo erectus* lived on the savanna in a climate that was cool and dry. Plant-based foods were limited; our fossil ancestors began to hunt and scavenge. Given the scarcity of plants and lack of variety because of the Ice Age, animal protein consumption was a wise choice. Our mistake has been to assume that animal protein is better for us than plant protein and the reason for the increase in the size of our brain. In fact, when a variety of plants are included in one's diet, plant protein is equal in quality to animal protein.

A big brain evolves when necessary. Our brains are 2% of our body weight, yet require 20%-25% of our metabolic energy; only need would justify the use of so much energy. Mammals, because of increased social interaction, tend to have larger brains than reptiles and fish of comparable size. Primates, living in large, complex social groups, have brains that are on average threes times bigger than those of other mammals, though all primates save the insectivorous tarsier are primarily vegetarian.

Over the past 6-7 million years, various genetic mutations in our fossil ancestors contributed to a bigger brain by increasing blood flow to the carotid artery and hence the brain; growth of the cerebral cortex; transfer of more glucose from muscles to the brain. Our magnificent hands evolved, which presented opportunities for creativity and inventions that made a larger brain desirable.

Between 2.4 to 5.3 million years ago, genetic mutations caused the jaws of our fossil ancestors to become smaller and weaker than those of other great apes, leaving room in the skull for the brain to eventually enlarge to four times the size of a chimpanzee's brain. The human skull doesn't close until one is fully adult. Other mutations led to more interconnections between our brain cells. Our fossil ancestors lost the air sacs on vocal tracts present in other great apes, and speech became possible. The brains of chimps and other apes are capable of language, but their vocal apparatus isn't suitable for speaking. The FOXP2 gene, associated with learning and language, appeared. Language led to more social complexity and the need for a larger brain. The control of fire and invention of hunting weapons likewise brought about complex social dynamics, necessitating a bigger brain. (The genetic mutations are listed in "15 Tweaks".)

We became bipedal. The bipedal stance resulted in a narrow birth canal, smaller birth size, and therefore an extended youth, when socialization and learning take place. This led to a thicker neocortex; the neocortex is associated with creativity, problem solving, reason, remembering and consciousness. (The critically endangered long-beaked echidna of Papua, New Guinea—the oldest surviving modern mammal species, dating back 120 million years—has an even thicker neocortex, comprising half of its brain!)

1.5 million-500,000 years ago the brain of our fossil ancestors doubled in size as tools became more sophisticated and as they learned to control fire; it doubled again the past 200,000 years since *Homo sapiens* appeared.

Taller, more massive human bodies coincided with a shift to increased animal protein consumption, therefore people have mistakenly concluded that animal protein is preferable to plant protein. However, eating more plant protein, provided that a variety of plants is consumed, allows one to reach one's optimal weight and height (*The China Study*, 102-3).

Alongside altruism, generosity and kindness, there is the potential for selfishness, arrogance, cruelty and lust for power within us. Selfishness and arrogance and ignorance have brought about crises that threaten life on Earth.

160,000 years ago the human population was small. In the last 150,000 years it has grown from around 50,000 to 7.3 billion. We are all closely related—one large, dysfunctional family. As humans spread out from the tropics and subtropics, skin color changed. Lighter skin allows one to absorb more sunlight and obtain more vitamin D, while darker skin protects one from too much sun. Only a handful of genes are responsible for skin color and other racial characteristics, but still there is racism. We have taken important steps away from racism in the United States since the Civil War; we can do the same with speciesism.

80,000 to 100,000 years ago humans developed symbolic thinking—we transform experience into symbols, expressed in words, words that may camouflage truth. For example, 'murder', with its moral condemnation, is restricted to members of our own species; we harvest/cull/ hunt/fish nonhuman animals. Such morally neutral terms used to describe killing obscure an obligation to treat our nonhuman animal family with kindness and compassion— they cement anthropocentric values. An animal is commonly referred to as 'it', like an inanimate object. Legally, animals are considered property; 'property' is defined as a thing or things belonging to someone, a 'thing' is defined as an object.

Human anatomy and physiology are designed for eating plants. The word 'omnivore' covers a lot of territory, as insects and worms and cows are all animals. We are omnivores to the extent that we can eat insects, invertebrates and small vertebrates such as frogs. Without hunting weapons, knives and fire, we would need to scavenge larger animals like cows and pigs, and such a choice wouldn't be necessary or healthy when a variety of plants are available. We lack talons or claws, we are not built to chase after prey.

True predators like cats and dogs are equipped with excellent night vision, keen hearing and a remarkable sense of smell. Our jaws cannot crush bones, our mouths are small and comparatively weak. Our canines are for display; they are not big enough to tear a part a medium-size or larger animal. Try killing a cow or pig with your bare hands and canines and eating the raw flesh. Our molars and premolars are designed to chew plants rather than slice through flesh, and our tongues cannot scrape flesh from bones. Our saliva contains amylase, an enzyme that breaks down carbohydrates. There is 95% less hydrochloric acid present in the human stomach than in a carnivore's stomach; hydrochloric acid helps dissolve animal flesh and bones. Human intestines are five times longer than those of carnivores, a length necessary to process plant fiber but not animal flesh. Autopsies sometimes reveal rancid animal flesh that had impacted on a person's intestinal wall for decades. (I know this because I typed autopsies for a time to help pay my way through college.)

A carnivore's powerful jaws open wide to catch the animal. The temporalis muscle of the upper jaw can suffocate prey and crush bones, the masseter muscle of the lower jaw help to cut flesh. Carnivore canine teeth are big.

Their molars and premolars lack flattened surfaces with cusps for chewing; instead, they have carnassials.

A carnivore's collarbone is smaller than a human collarbone and attached in a way that lets the predator chase after prey. Bones of the lower front and back limbs (the ulna and fibula) are well developed in carnivores to aid in running, and the ulna is locked to the radius for strength. Wrist bones have fused into a scapho-lunar bone in carnivores to soften the impact from running and to help the animal wrestle with prey. The retractile claws of cats grasp prey, the digging claws of canids let them bury prey for later consumption (*PEM,* 480-81). We have trichromatic vision that evolved to help us distinguish ripe fruits; carnivores have dichromatic vision.

Throughout the animal kingdom, anatomy and physiology correspond to diet. The upper jaw of the Atlantic sailfish is like a sword, to knife through shoals of fish and to daze/mutilate prey. The huge beak of a toucan provides it with access to fruit at the ends of branches. The proventriculus is larger in in raptors, the gizzard is larger in seed-eating birds. Ruminants regurgitate nutrient-poor grasses to digest them again. The manatee has a 150-foot intestine that processes the high-fiber seagrass it consumes. The giraffe's one-and-a-half foot prehensile tongue reaches acacia leaves among the thorns. Snakes have hinged jaws and stretchable skin that enable them to consume whole animals, and their stomach and liver enlarge to digest the prey. The exceedingly long tongue of the panther chameleon shoots out to grasp an unsuspecting insect. Komodo dragons have large serrated teeth to capture prey. Sharks are able to taste small amounts of blood in the water to find prey, and electrical sense organs on their snout let them locate prey in darkness. Baleen plates attached to the rooftop of a baleen whale's mouth filter plankton from seawater. A butterfly unfurls a tubular proboscis to suck nectar from flowers. Every animal has an anatomy and digestive system appropriate for its diet.

Though our bodies can digest animal-based foods, it isn't necessary for us to consume any animal flesh or dairy. The human body is hardy enough to take a lot of abuse. With surgeries and medication (sometimes even without), a person whose diet includes animal flesh and dairy may live a long life. However, problems with animal protein consumption extend far beyond personal health, to deforestation, climate change, mass extinction, animal cruelty and more. We have claimed land for ourselves, our crops, and for livestock grazing, killing immense numbers of wildlife. Our cruelty to factory farm animals and wildlife is heinous. An organic whole foods vegan diet is the only diet that respects life on Earth.

## EVOLUTION AND RELIGION

Fossils provide abundant evidence of evolution. Different species have existed at different times. Some transitional fossils exist, like the micro-raptor dinosaur with feathers. DNA links us to all other living organisms—we share 200 genes with unicellular life, and we share nearly all of our DNA with the other great apes.

Islands such as Madagascar and the Galapagos show evolution in action. Lemurs rafted to Madagascar tens of millions of years ago, evolving into species seen nowhere else. The Galapagos Islands, too, have unique species; for instance, finch species have developed beaks suitable to food sources on a particular island.

Plate tectonics, continental drift and climate change have effected the Earth throughout history; some species have gone extinct while new ones appeared. (This doesn't excuse us for the current anthropogenic climate change and human-caused mass extinction.)

Kindness is a central message of all major religions. For those who believe that humans have dominion over other animals, dominion can only mean stewardship—taking care of the Earth and all animals. Would God wish mankind to harm or destroy His creations? Would God wish for people to eat foods that put them at risk of cancer, heart disease and more? Would God wish for deforestation, ocean acidification, and the human-caused climate change and mass extinction underway? Whether or not one accepts the theory of evolution, we must work together to save the animals, we must join together to take care of the Earth, setting aside our differences.

## CLIMATE CHANGE

The Earth's atmosphere consists of nitrogen (78.09%), oxygen (20.95%), argon (nearly 1%), and greenhouse gases, chiefly water ($H_2O$), carbon dioxide ($CO_2$), methane ($CH_4$), nitrous oxide ($N_2O$) and ozone ($O_3$). These greenhouse gases, though present in small amounts, can affect climate greatly. Eric Grimsrud has written a clear, concise book to educate the general public, *Thoughts of a Scientist, Citizen, and Grandpa on Climate Change*, and Wikipedia articles on atmospheric methane, greenhouse gases, climate change and global warming provide charts, graphs, and hundreds of scholarly references. Wikipedia articles are a splendid resource for nonscientists that desire to understand climate change. Continually revised, they provide up-to-date data; this is especially important regarding methane, clouds and the ocean, all of which need to be better understood in relationship to climate change. Questionable information is flagged/removed. It is essential for people to move past confusion and denial of climate change to clarity and action.

Molecules composed of three or more atoms, such as water, carbon dioxide, methane and nitrous oxide, absorb infrared radiation (IR) the Earth releases to cool itself. (Molecules consisting of two atoms of different elements, for example, carbon monoxide, also absorb IR, but their contribution to global warming is negligible, for they are short-lived in the atmosphere.) Fossil fuels formed from the decomposition of living organisms over hundreds of millions of years. Burning fossil fuels releases carbon dioxide into the atmosphere, where it remains for up to a hundred years; 20% of $CO_2$ may remain in the atmosphere for thousands of years (Wiki/*Greenhouse gas*). Polar ice tells the story of warmer and cooler periods in the geological past; scientists have spent decades drilling into the ice to learn about climate changes the past 800,000 years. Increased atmospheric greenhouse gases set in motion a sequence of climate-altering events lasting hundreds of years beyond the time they are present in the atmosphere. For example, ice reflects sunlight, therefore, when ice melts, the Earth becomes hotter. Global warming causes droughts and fires that cause more global warming, creating a spiral. This is why we mustn't postpone actions to mitigate climate change.

The amount of the carbon-13 isotope present in the atmosphere cannot be from volcanic activity or the ocean; in addition, the present amounts of atmospheric carbon-13 and carbon-14 have never occurred before; they began to increase at the start of the Industrial Revolution (*Thoughts, 8)*.

The United Nations Intergovernmental Panel on Climate Change (IPCC) reported in 2014 that scientists are more than 95% certain that most global warming is happening because of the increase in human-induced greenhouse gas emissions (www.livescience.com and Wiki/*Global warming)*. They have carefully researched alternative explanations, and there has been much debate. Scientists are dedicated to finding the truth; they have amazing technology to aid them. It is rash to ignore their findings, extraordinarily dangerous to deny climate change.

Burning fossils fuels and deforestation, both increased by human population growth, are central reasons for climate change. Most significant of all is the livestock sector. In 2009 Robert Goodland, a senior environmental advisor to the World Bank Group, and Jeff Anhang wrote in "Livestock and Climate Change" that the livestock sector (raising/killing the animals, animal feed and distribution of animal feed, animal flesh, dairy and byproducts) is responsible for more than half of human-induced greenhouse gas emissions. If commercial fishing were included in calculations of greenhouse gas emissions, then the animal protein sector would be responsible for an even larger percentage.

Animal protein production uses eight times as much fossil fuel as plant agriculture. Farm animals produce 9% of global $CO_2$ emissions, 35-40% of global human-induced methane, and 64% of global nitrous oxide, mainly from fertilizer use (Wiki/*Agriculture; Methane; Greenhouse gas*). Over a hundred-year period nitrous oxide has 298 times more impact per unit weight than carbon dioxide (Wiki/*Greenhouse gas*); over 500 years it has 153 times more impact.

More people are adopting an animal-based diet, and people are choosing to consume larger amounts of animal protein—American citizens are among the biggest consumers of animal flesh and dairy. The United Nations Environment Programme (unep.org) estimates that methane from livestock will increase 60% by 2030 should current practices and consumptive patterns continue (Wiki/ *Agriculture*). Antibiotics used to decrease the amount of methane produced during digestion in ruminants destroy beneficial bacteria essential to digestion, and so are an unkind, unhealthy option. The best course of action is to stop eating animal flesh and dairy.

More than 200 experts working with the United Nations concur that up to 80% of tropical deforestation in the Amazon rainforest is to transform the land into grazing land for livestock (planetsave.com) and to grow food, much of it for the animals people eat. As trees disappear, there is naturally less photosynthesis, and therefore more $CO_2$.

Atmospheric methane has increased around 150% since the Industrial Age began and more than 30% in the past four decades. After a plateau during the 1990s and early 2000s, the level of atmospheric methane began to increase again in 2007. Methane affects climate change directly and also indirectly, by contributing to ozone formation. Atmospheric methane reacts with the hydroxyl radical (OH). Increased methane will deplete OH; methane would then remain longer in the atmosphere, increasing its global warming potential. It is difficult to measure exactly how much more potent a greenhouse gas methane is than carbon dioxide, but it is currently estimated to be from 72 to 100 times more potent the first years, eventually becoming equivalent. Chemical reactions cause atmospheric methane to oxidize into water and carbon dioxide, which aren't included in methane's global warming potential, and because oxidation of methane also contributes to ozone production, methane's global warming potential could be at least double current estimates (Wiki/*Greenhouse gas*).

The sea temperature is rising at an accelerated rate. On the ocean floor of the Arctic Sea lies a two and a half gigaton deposit of frozen methane hydrate that has begun to rise as the sea ice melts; it will eventually enter the atmosphere. Warmer temperatures are also exposing methane in the permafrost, posing the threat of a worst-case scenario, "runaway" global warming, as it would lead to the production of more methane in wetlands, for instance (*Thoughts,* 4). The relatively short time methane lasts in the atmosphere (8.5 or 12 years, depending on which factors are used in calculation) is a reason to adopt an organic vegan now, as this could bring about a rapid decline in atmospheric greenhouse gas concentrations in the near future.

In addition to livestock grazing and agriculture, manufacturing and packaging are reasons for deforestation.

Many people fail to recycle cardboard, plywood and paper products. Global distribution of products causes greenhouse gas emissions. Owning a large home (or homes) means that more resources are used, there is more deforestation, more fossil fuels are used to heat/cool the home(s), and there is more habitat loss, leading to more extinctions.

Past climate changes were caused in part by plate tectonics, continental drift, and by cyclic variations in the tilt of the Earth's axis toward the sun (the Milankovitch cycle) that result in alternating periods of cooler and warmer temperatures. During the Permian-Triassic Extinction, many volcanic eruptions contributed to global warming. There were no polar ice caps during that time, and the sea level was much higher than now. When temperatures are cooler, ice and snow reflect sunlight to further cool the planet. The Sun can't be blamed for the steep increase in atmospheric carbon dioxide the last four decades, and volcanic eruptions currently contribute only 1% of what human-induced greenhouse gas emissions do. The desire to deny global warming leads people to set aside common sense.

Since 1750 atmospheric $CO_2$ has increased from 280 ppm to 400 ppm, after being constant for 2,000 years; much of the increase happened in the last four decades (Wiki/ *Greenhouse gas*). 75% of the increase in the last 20 years is from fossil fuel burning, the rest mainly from deforestation. The yearly rate of increase, 2 ppm (parts per million), is approximately 100 times faster than during any period of global warming the past 750,000 years (*Thoughts,* 13). The high point during previous warmer periods in this time frame was 280 ppm. Levels could reach 541-970 ppm by 2100, according to an IPCC report (Wiki/*Global warming*). From 1850 to 2008 the United States contributed to 28.5% of energy-related $CO_2$ emissions (Wiki/*Greenhouse gas*)—a reason for us to lead the world in reducing greenhouse gas emissions. Worldwide, human-induced greenhouse gas emissions could rise 25-90% by 2030, compared to 2000 (Wiki/*Greenhouse gas*).

Storing carbon dioxide in the deep ocean isn't an option, for it increases ocean acidification. Carbon capture and sequestration are being explored as a partial solution; however, there are likely to be unforeseen consequences such as lethal leaks. There remain, too, the unsustainable use of resources, deforestation, the many ways we harm marine life, cruelty, death and extinction to animals and plants, the health risks of animal protein consumption and human population growth.

There is no need for destructive lifestyle and diet choices, no need for us to harm and destroy species upon species. We are one family with all animals; it is wrong to set aside moral considerations concerning them in the pursuit of money, or because the taste of animal flesh and dairy gives pleasure. When we come to view money from the perspective of kindness and compassion, we will solve problems everywhere.

To stop rising temperatures, anthropogenic greenhouse gas emissions must be reduced by 80% compared to peak level emissions (Wiki/*Global warming*). It is possible and healthy to achieve an 80% reduction by widespread adoption—now—of an organic vegan diet, a prompt shift to clean energy such solar, driving vehicles with low fuel consumption, buying less, living more simply, building smaller homes and traveling less. Tourism is responsible for around half of global traffic movements (Wiki/*Greenhouse gas*). Take fewer trips, tent camp, travel closer to home and/or travel to places to volunteer (for example, planting trees, or helping to educate people about climate change/mass extinction/organic farming/vegan diet). Combined, these changes can make a tremendous difference, together we can change the world!

The last 39 years, including 2015, have been warmer than the average 20th century temperature (Wiki/*Global warming*). In 2012 Munich Re, a reinsurance firm, wrote that from 1980-2011 weather-related disasters in North America nearly quintupled (www.munichre.com). Droughts, heat waves, forest fires and floods are more numerous; 2014 was the hottest year on record (nasa.gov/press), and globally, July, 2015, was the hottest month ever recorded (ncdc.coaa.gov/sotc). Records were set in 2016 as well. The temperature has risen 0.8-0.9°C/1.5°F in the last 50 years (Wiki/*Global warming*). Scientists have also found evidence of temperature spikes in the distant past, when the temperature suddenly rose many degrees, to remain high for hundreds of years (*Years of Living Dangerously*); there is no reason to trust that it will continue to climb at a steady pace. We must wake up.

Though the impact of climate change is commonly viewed in terms of the economy and humanity, there are calamitous consequences for animals and plants. Over time climate change will likely be a central reason for mass extinction, destroying much life that evolved over hundreds of millions of years. A rise of more than 2°C/3.6°F will lead to a phenomenal number of extinctions of both plant and animal species. Thomas Lovejoy, a professor of Science and Public Policy at George Mason University, wrote in an Op-Ed for the New York Times January 21, 2013, that a rise of 2°C will destroy all coral reefs, most of the coniferous forests in western North America, and much of the Amazon rain forest—habitats for most wildlife and marine species. A 10% chance of a rise of 6°C/10.8°F by 2100 has been forecast by leading climate scientists (<u>independent.co.uk/ environment/climate-change</u>). In 2010 the National Research Council's Panel on Advancing the Science of Climate Change estimated an increase of up to 4.8°C/8.6°F (Wiki/<u>Global warming</u>). I haven't seen estimates that extend beyond 2100, but the temperature rises listed above are probably just the beginning.

Global warming leads to sea ice melt, rising sea levels, and warmer ocean temperatures. Rising sea levels guarantee greater storm surges. Should the temperature rise 2°C relative to pre-industrial levels, the sea level could rise up to 4m/13' (Wiki/*Global warming*), from thermal expansion of sea water and glacier melt. As the Western Antarctic Ice Sheet melts, the sea level will rise 3m/10' or more (Wiki/ *Western Antarctic Ice Sheet)*, and when/if the Greenland ice sheet melts, the sea could rise another 7.5m/23.5' (Wiki/ *Global warming)*. In 2016 scientists discovered that the Totten Glacier in Eastern Antarctica was melting. Warm sea water is finding its way inland, increasing the part of the glacier resting on water instead of rock. This could result in an additional 2m/6.5' sea level rise this century. In the early

Pliocene, around 5.2 million years ago, global temperatures were only 2-3°C higher than today, and the sea level was up to 25 m/81.25' higher.

Scientists now understand reasons for a seeming plateau of global warming in recent years (latimes.com/science/ sciencenow). When previously missing data from polar regions is included, global warming is evident. Also, the deep waters of the Atlantic Ocean have absorbed more heat than anticipated, lessening the rise of surface temperatures. Finally, an extended pattern of warmer/cooler temperatures in the Pacific Ocean, called the Pacific Decadal Oscillation, has been in a cooler phase for the last decade, temporally resulting in cooler temperatures, especially in Eurasia. Recent data indicates that the pattern may be shifting to a warmer phase. There remains much to be understood about the effects of greenhouse gas emissions on the ocean and about the effect of clouds on global warming.

A drop in gas prices in recent years led people in the United States to rush to purchase large SUVs and trucks. For the most part, the vehicles are neither electric nor hybrid, and many are used for personal use. Often there is only a driver and perhaps one passenger to be seen in the SUV. Driving a vehicle with high fuel consumption increases atmospheric $CO_2$. Increased demand for gas and oil may lead to fracking and drilling in the Arctic, both environmentally risky. We act indifferent to the fate of life on Earth. Oblivious and complacent, we are sleepwalking to a cataclysm of our own making. Each one of us must find the clarity and courage to do the right thing.

The tide may be turning. On November 4, 2016, the Paris Climate Change Accord will go into effect. Though not legally binding, nations will attempt to keep the temperature from rising above 2°C/3.6°F; however, replacing fossil fuels with nuclear power is reckless until/unless there is a safe way to dispose of nuclear waste. Bill Gates has mobilized billionaires to fund the exploration of new energies. The Obama administration has proposed regulations to curb methane waste from oil and gas production on public lands over the next 10 years that would reduce levels to 45% of what they were in 2012. The large majority of millennials want there to be mostly renewable energy used by 2030. Nevertheless, it is imperative that each person understand the impact of diet, lifestyle choices and human population growth on all life. Only as each person changes will we stop deforestation, the harm we bring to the ocean, the killing and cruelty to animals everywhere, the use of too many resources—all that we now do that is destroying life on Earth.

The United States is largely responsible for the current climate change; since the Industrial Revolution began, we have contributed about 30% of human-induced greenhouse gas emissions. Though China now emits more greenhouse gases than the United States, we are simply outsourcing the manufacturing of many of our goods to China and therefore bear much responsibility. Deforestation in South America and Southeast Asia provides us with cheap hamburgers and paper goods and palm oil for our snacks and soaps, etc. The United States, with less than 5% of the world's population, creates one half of global waste, uses one third of the world's paper and around a quarter of the world's oil, coal and aluminum (*Use it*). Our American way of life would require four Earths to be sustainable—we are ravaging the planet to live the way we do, and we are robbing the youth and their children of Nature.

All arguments in support of doubt or denial of anthropocentric climate change collapse under scrutiny. However, during the 2016 Presidential campaign, little mention has been made of climate change. A 2016 Pew poll of conservative Republicans found that the large majority deny that climate change is occurring, and claim that, if it does exist, it's not human-caused, and that even if it is occurring, they can't do anything to stop it. Skepticism and ignorance misdirect focus from a crisis that grows every day as we ignore it. The consequences of denying anthropogenic climate change could not be more tragic. It is time to spread awareness—passionately, persistently, peacefully.

Most Americans believe that material possessions are essential for happiness. Accumulation of things, often big things (big cars, big homes, big yachts, big RVs, etc.) is socially encouraged and condoned. Yet the happiest person I remember seeing is an Indian rickshaw runner interviewed in a documentary about happiness. He lives in a slum, runs barefoot all day, sometimes runs in heavy rain, is subjected to rudeness by passengers, but he seems radiantly happy. He says the reasons for his happiness are that he returns to his family every night to share a meal, and he enjoys his neighbors. He feels lucky. Given the impact a materialistic lifestyle has on nature, his point of view is inspiring (which is not to say that poverty is a prerequisite for happiness).

The habit of gratitude is life-transforming. For at least 30 consecutive days, say out loud 100 things for which you are grateful, such as a stranger's smile or a California poppy blooming; it will be one of the best gifts you ever give yourself.

Climate change, when not triggered by an asteroid smashing into the planet, can take place over thousands of years, even much longer periods. However, most predictions for the current global warming focus on the impact only to the end of this century. Even during this mere moment of geological time, catastrophic events are expected to occur. Hunger, war, disease, panic and poverty may prevail. Tens or hundreds of millions or more people could need to relocate in the coming century or two. Where will they go? Hotter temperatures, droughts, fires, winds, floods and heavy rains could make much of the planet uninhabitable. No one can wish this for the young people, for the children. We must wake up.

The United States must lead in mitigating global warming and saving plant and animal species from extinction. Our insouciance towards climate change places an unbearable burden on young people, on all life. We have been acting as recklessly as drunken teenagers taking a joyride at night in a convertible, speeding 100 mph down a dark highway, driving straight to a precipice. Only we are destroying much life on Earth as we careen to catastrophe.

It is heartbreaking to reflect upon all that is likely to disappear unless we change now. Consider the coral reefs. Coral reefs occur worldwide in sunlit, clear, shallow tropical and subtropical seas. They are formed from the accumulation of limestone skeletons of hard corals, with mollusks and echinoderms adding their skeletons. Algae and other organisms help to fasten sand and coral particles together.

Coral species have diverse shapes and sizes and colors. There are elk horn corals, stag horn corals, finger, corals, golfball corals. There are daisy corals, with tentacles arranged like daisy petals, and sea fans resembling plants with large leaves. There are white sea whips, and pulse corals with featherlike tentacles that continually open and shut. Branching carnation corals add colors—red, yellows, oranges—to the reef, as do giant anemones with purple-tipped tentacles, and Mediterranean red corals. Cup-shaped dendrophyllid corals may cover a wide area, expanding golden orange tentacles at night (*Ocean*, 152-61).

Symbiotic zooxanthellae living within corals and providing their glorious colors must be in surface water to photosynthesize; they cannot survive rising sea levels. The sea level rose 13-24" on the East coast of the United States last century. Worldwide  the sea level is forecast to rise a meter/3+ feet or more by 2100; however, the sea level has been rising faster than models have estimated (Wiki/*Global warming*). Also, predictions haven't included recent findings regarding the Western Antarctic Ice Sheet (WAIS). From 1958 to 2012 the WAIS warmed 2.4°C. On May 12, 2014, two teams of scientists announced that they had found evidence the WAIS is past saving, even were we to take immediate steps to reduce climate change (Wiki/*Western Antarctic Ice Sheet*). The sea beneath the glaciers is warming, loosening glaciers from the bedrock that had held them secure, hence the glaciers are moving more quickly to the sea, and more ice is breaking off.

When stressed, as happens with even slightly higher ocean temperatures over a few years, corals expel the zooxanthellae. This is called bleaching, because the corals turn white. Repeated bleaching, such has been occurring, leads to death by starvation.

The ocean is a carbon sink, and increased amounts of $CO_2$ are resulting in ocean acidification. The ocean surface pH has dropped from approximately 8.2 in 1750 to around 8.1 in 2000, and it is estimated to drop another 0.3-0.4 units by 2100, lower than any time the past 2 million years (Wiki/*Global warming*). Ocean acidification is causing the calcareous shells and skeletons of corals, crustaceans, some mollusks and echinoderms, bryozoans and other marine life to weaken, become thin, dissolve, or not form at all. Ocean acidification puts all marine life at risk, for many of the animals listed above are central to the oceanic food web.

Perhaps a million species in numerous phyla dwell in coral reefs, dependent upon the reefs for survival. Many of the 15,000 sponge species inhabit coral reefs. Some remarkably beautiful worms can be found in coral reefs. Many mollusks live in reefs, including giant clams and the flamingo tongue. Reef-dwelling crustaceans include the beautiful little anemone shrimp, the peacock mantis shrimp, and various crab and lobster species. Pink lace bryozoans live in reefs. Sand dollars, sea urchins, starfish and feather stars are echinoderm residents of reefs, and colonies of sea squirts can be found there.

The whale shark, the world's largest fish, spends time near coral reefs feeding on plankton and small fish. Other sharks found in or near reefs include white sharks, blue sharks, tiger sharks, whitecap reef sharks and scalloped hammerhead sharks. Spotted eagle rays and manta rays swim in or near reefs.

The number and variety of ray-finned coral reef fish is astounding. The male ribbon eel is bright blue with canary yellow jaws. The brown-and-red camouflaged reef lizardfish has a mouth that opens wide enough to swallow sizable fish whole. Shoals of reddish whitecap soldierfish swim at night in Indo-Pacific reefs. Atlantic flying fish live in tropical and temperate waters. Long, thin trumpetfish (up to 1m/3') hide among corals. The pygmy seahorse is camouflaged to look like the sea fans where it hides. Groups of razorfish swim vertically, facing downward. The red-striped lion fish is a nocturnal hunter in reefs.

Many reef fish have deep bodies. Some, such the exquisite queen angelfish, are thin, enabling them to move in and out of the corals. Fish dwelling in shallow waters often have vibrant colors. There are golden orange fish like the fairy basslet or the ring-tailed cardinal fish, polka-dotted harlequin sweetlips and common bluestripe snappers. Mandarin fish have extravagant orange, yellow, blue, green and turquoise patterns.

Green turtles, hawksbill turtles, Kemp's Ridley turtles and loggerhead turtles are reef inhabitants. Snakes found in coral reefs include olive sea snakes, turtle-headed snakes, leaf-scaled sea snakes and yellow-lipped sea kraits. Herons, egrets, ospreys and other seabirds fly over coral reefs, and bottlenose dolphins swim nearby.

By mid-century, unless we change now, all coral reefs will experience bleaching, and repeated bleaching, as has been happening to many reefs already, leads to death. The astonishing abundance, diversity and unsurpassable beauty of coral reefs are to be treasured beyond all the gold in the world. Once they are destroyed, only weeds and jellyfish will remain.

In 2012 the Arctic ocean summer ice was about half what it had been on average in the 1980s and 1990s. Much of the thicker, older ice that polar bears and walruses use as platforms is gone. Many mother polar bears with cubs are forced to swim 12 days in search of sea ice, and they drown. Others grow weak with hunger, pregnancy becomes too challenging, cubs frequently die.

Rising sea temperatures lead to less oxygen (2% less oxygen/1°C temperature rise), while causing fish metabolism to speed up, which makes them need more, not less, oxygen. Countless fish will die as ocean deoxygenation continues to increase. Deoxygenation has led to a 40% decline in phytoplankton the last 50 years.

The Antarctic krill population is less than 20% of what it was only a few decades ago (*Ocean*, 293). Krill eat algae that grow on the underside of the ice, and their larvae find safety in cracks in the ice, ice that is melting. Krill are a primary food for blue whales, sea birds, penguins and many fish species.

Atmospheric greenhouse gases are affecting air currents like the El Niño-Southern Oscillation, causing more frequent, longer lasting, severe droughts in some areas. The 2000-2004 drought in the central United States was one of the worst in 800 years (sciencedaily.com/releases). In the Southwestern US, rain-bearing cloud formations are shifting north. Drought is forecast for as long as global warming continues, or a very long time indeed. 50 years ago in the western United States, there were only a few summer days when the temperature rose above 100°F. Now 30-60 days/year temperatures above 100°F happen in numerous western states (*Years*). There have also been extreme droughts in parts of South America and the Mideast. Worldwide cloud formations are shifting poleward, where they cannot reflect as much sunlight, thus exacerbating global warming.

Some places, including parts of Europe, the northeastern United States and Canada, will become cooler despite overall global warming. As sea ice melts, deep sea currents change, affecting climate. The Atlantic Conveyor, that has given Europe a warmer climate, may shut down as Arctic sea ice melts (*Ocean*, 63).

Droughts and heat waves cause hotter, more extensive, longer burning forest fires. Heat from forest fires and ensuing erosion can prevent regrowth for up to a thousand years. California has experienced some of the worst forest fires in its history; during the summer of 2015, there were dozens of fires. The American Geophysical Union reported that higher temperatures made the drought and fires from 15% to 20% worse; higher temperatures suck water from plants and soil. They also reported that in the decades after 2050 there could be almost uninterrupted drought in California.

Drought weakens trees, while bark beetles thrive. North American forest bark beetle infestations destroyed 26.8 million acres between 1997-2010, leaving little food for grizzlies and other animals (*Wildlife in a Warming World* [WWW], www.nwf.org). The larvae eat the trees. Dead trees easily catch on fire. Bristlecone pines—the oldest living organisms—and giant sequoias are at risk in the coming century, as are the piñon trees in the Southwest, where tree skeletons have become a common sight; piñons can survive drought but not higher temperatures, too. Wildlife are left without food. Worldwide many insect populations will increase with global warming.

For wildlife, heat waves, droughts and fires can mean thirst/starvation/death/possible extinction. They may lose everything—shelter, water and food sources. Bears, big horn sheep, foxes, elk, moose, deer, squirrels, picas, marmots, cougars, coyotes, many bird species, and countless other animal species die. Ash falling on streams suffocates fish and kills the invertebrates on the riverbed. Animals seek shade from the heat, and they don't eat enough to survive the following winter (*WWW*). Ticks thrive to torment moose, elk and deer. They rub some of their fur off to rid themselves of the ticks, then freeze to death the following winter (*WWW*). As rivers dry up, migrating birds dependent upon them die. Frogs die when ponds dry up. Butterfly species face extinction locally.

In the Midwest, climate change is causing heavier rains or severe droughts, floods, winds and severe storms, all destroying immense numbers of wildlife. Flooding fills rivers with fertilizers, pesticides and herbicides that kill fresh water fish, then flow into the ocean to destroy marine life. Wetland bird habitats are destroyed. Invasive plant species crowd out ones that wildlife depend on for survival (*WWW*). Rising sea levels attributable to climate change threaten East Coast wildlife as well as people—birds lose habitats and turtles lose egg-laying beaches, for example.

The financial costs of climate change are already tens of billions of dollars a year. Sea level rising a foot or more on the eastern Atlantic coast of the United States the last century resulted in $60-70 billion damage from Hurricane Sandy. The melting of the Western Antarctic Ice Sheet will cost trillions of dollars, as will melting ice in the Arctic and Greenland.

Predictions for what will happen to humanity by the end of this century are apocalyptic, even without factoring in the methane from warming permafrost or the WAIS melting. Glacier retreat and disappearance will affect hundreds of millions of people globally, causing floods then extreme droughts in coming decades. Deaths attributable to climate change were 5 million worldwide in 2010, with an estimated 6 million in 2030.

The climate change crisis is so great one can slip into hopelessness, but hope generates enthusiasm, hope stimulates creativity. To give up hope before trying with all one's heart is to betray the young people, children, animals and plants. Every choice makes a difference, for better or worse. Choose to hope. In order to mitigate climate change, the first, foremost changes one should make are to adopt an organic vegan diet and to live simply, sustainably.

## DEFORESTATION

We are destroying tropical rain forests, where half of the world's plant and animal species live. Atmospheric $CO_2$ increases when forests are destroyed, especially those on peat in Southeast Asia. Trees transpire, releasing water vapor into the atmosphere to form clouds that bring rain or snow.

Deforestation leads to droughts, forest fires and heat waves, as happened in Brazil in the 1990s, and the forest fires destroy surrounding rain forest.

Rainforest trees, rather than the soil, contain the nutrients; they also hold water and capture heat. When their leaves fall, they provide the soil with fertilizer. Deforestation causes the topsoil to be carried away in floods or by the wind; it can take up to 500 years to replace one inch of topsoil. The soil turn into hard dirt. The microbial communities of the pasture land that replaces the rain forest are different from those of rain forests and less durable. Within only a few years, livestock can no longer graze on the land, and crops don't grow. The farmers burn more forests to create new grazing land and to grow food crops, setting in motion a cycle of death/destruction/escalating climate change. Until recently, one acre of South American rain forest was being set on fire every second. Though the rate has slowed, the rain forests could still disappear in the coming decades. Additionally, as temperatures warm, trees grow more slowly and therefore use less carbon dioxide; this accelerates global warming.

Lelia and Sebastiao Salgado have proved that it is possible to restore a rain forest. The trees on the ranch where Sebastiao Salgado grew up had been cut down. The waterfall disappeared, as did the wildlife. Persistent droughts replaced the rains. The couple devoted years to planting 250,000,000 trees. The rains, the waterfall returned. Jaguars and other wildlife found their way to the forest, which is now a National Park.

The Amazon Fund in Brazil is committed to reducing deforestation in the Amazon, and the Billion Tree Campaign had planted more than 12 billion trees worldwide as of 2012. China and Indonesia are making reforestation efforts. It would be wonderful for the United States to establish something similar to the Peace Corps to help reforest South America, Africa and Southeast Asia, as well as North American forests.

Imagine a world where rain forests are more important than eating animal flesh and dairy or owning a large home. Imagine a kind, compassionate world and act every day to create that world. Commit to using recycled paper products and to recycling plywood, cardboard and other paper products. Avoid products containing palm oil (unless it is sustainably farmed). Live simply, use as little lumber as possible.

Nature affords us beauty, delight, sanity. Nature gives us an escape from the pressures to conform and compete and from preoccupations with status and wealth that dominate human concerns, yet like a steamroller, we are squashing Nature. Caught up in the craziness of a misdirected society, we devalue what is most essential, viewing our might as entitlement to destroy life whenever and wherever and however we desire. We fail to see that other species matter, we forget to treasure life. Humankind is not above nature. We need the pollinators and seed dispersers, we need forests, we need nature for its unparalleled beauty and for our peace of mind. We must learn to act from reverence for life rather than selfishness.

## MASS EXTINCTION, THE KILLING FIELD

There is half the wildlife there was 40 years ago, and most marine fish have been killed. A World Wide Fund for Nature (WWF) *Living Planet Report 2014* studied over 10,000 representative global populations of some 3,000 species. Worldwide there was overall a 52% decline in wildlife from 1970 to 2010, with a 76% decline in freshwater fish, frogs and shorebirds. Freshwater species are the most vulnerable to extinction because of human-caused pollution, human population growth and increased water use nearly double the increase of human population. Land species declined 38%, marine species 39%. The elephant population has decreased 60% since 2002, and 60% of all large herbivores are at risk of extinction. The big cats and hyenas that prey on them will likely become extinct as their prey disappear. The sharpest decline in wildlife populations are found in tropical ecosystems. Because people living in rich countries in temperate zones outsource food and resources such as timber from poor tropical countries, we all bear responsibility.

In the past several hundred years, the rate of extinction increased twelvefold, and it continues to escalate. Most biologists believe that a sixth mass extinction, caused by human activity, is in progress. Deforestation, fishing, hunting, human population growth and diet/lifestyle choices are annihilating much life on Earth. Within the coming decades, 25-50% of all mammal species and a third of all bird species may disappear. 250 million years ago the Permian-Triassic Extinction annihilated 90% of all species in 60,000 years or more, and that is viewed as quickly in geological terms. The current extinction rate, perhaps one hundred times faster than during previous mass extinctions, leaves many animals too little time to adapt to climate change.

The Permian-Triassic Mass Extinction was the greatest mass extinction until now. Plate tectonics moved land masses. Tremendous volcanic eruptions in Siberia, covering a million square miles, heated rocks, releasing enormous amounts of carbon dioxide. The ocean temperature rose. Parts of the ocean had no oxygen, and marine life disappeared there. Increased carbon dioxide caused ocean acidification. Sea levels rose. Coral reefs disappeared, and it took 20 million years for them to be fully re-established. As the ocean food web collapsed, a mass extinction occurred— only 4% of marine animal species survived. Currently, increased atmospheric greenhouse gases are causing climate changes similar to the global warming brought about by the Permian volcanic eruptions.

The International Union for Conservation of Nature (IUCN) Red List of endangered species includes those at risk of becoming extinct in the near and medium future. The Red List divides species into the following categories: Extinct (EX); Extinct in the Wild (EW); Critically Endangered (CR)— facing an extremely high risk of extinction in the immediate future; Endangered (EN)—facing a very high risk of extinction in the near future; Vulnerable (VU)—facing a high risk of extinction in the medium term; Near-threatened (NT) —may be considered threatened in the near future; and Least Concern (LC)—no immediate threat to species' survival. The Bactrian camel, California condor, Chinese giant salamander, Hawaiian monk seal, mountain gorilla, red wolf, Sumatran rhinoceros and tiger are examples of critically endangered animals; the Asian elephant, Asiatic lion, blue whale, bonobo, Bornean orangutan, common chimpanzee, eastern lowland gorilla, giant panda, loggerhead sea turtle, Japanese crane, proboscis monkey, pygmy hippopotamus, snow leopard and numerous other splendid species are endangered. It is heart-rending.

40% of the world's species are currently considered at risk of extinction. Countless more will be threatened in the coming centuries and millennia. In the Americas, animal species at risk in the near future include the Florida panther, red wolf, Indiana bat, black-headed spider monkey, Geoffrey's spider monkey, Yucatan black howler monkey, golden lion tamarin, black lion tamarin, golden-headed tamarin and giant otter (this list isn't comprehensive). In Europe and northern Asia, the Siberian tiger, Iberian lynx, Amur leopard and other species are in grave danger of extinction. Magnificent African animals, including parrots, elephants, leopards, lions, primates, rhinos and hippos, are at risk of disappearing forever. The orangutans, gibbons, tigers, and many more species in Southeast Asia are in great peril. Manatees and dugongs are at risk. Amphibians, turtles, crocodilians and snakes face extinction. Butterfly, bee and bird species are in danger.

Coastal habitat loss is leading to extinctions. Rising sea levels will eliminate many animal habitats along coasts and in the shallow seas, especially coral reefs. Arctic sea ice is melting more and earlier from climate change. Small islands where turtles swim to lay their eggs will disappear with the rising sea level.

Mangrove swamps, important habitats for marine life, are being destroyed to make way for shrimp farms and to be replaced by hotels and marinas. The toxic effluent from the shrimp farms poisons coral reefs, as well as mangroves growing close by. Mangrove swamps protect coral reefs from silt buildup, and coral reefs protect mangrove swamps from tides. Hundreds of plant species grow in the trees' root systems. Fallen mangrove leaves become food for crabs, or are broken down by fungi and bacteria, to be consumed by shrimp and small fish, which are eaten by mollusks, worms, crustaceans and brittlestars, which are in turn consumed by larger fish. Reptiles, birds and mammals prey on fish. This food web is collapsing.

As the mangrove forests disappear, millions of North American migratory birds lose their winter habitat. Herons, egrets, anhingas, pelicans, greater flamingos, hummingbirds, storks, fish-eagles, spoonbills, toucans, kingfishers, hawks and other species have neither shelter nor sustenance. American crocodiles and Nile crocodiles, gharials, turtles, boa constrictors, iguanas, snakes and water monitor lizards lose home and food sources. Mammals, including manatees and dugongs, otters, spider monkeys, proboscis monkeys, Bengal tigers, Irrawaddy dolphins and many rodent species are at risk of extinction. Countless fish lose a nursery for their young, as well as their hunting ground, their home (*Ocean*, 130-35).

Birds everywhere are threatened, as discussed in the chapter on birds. Parrot species are endangered from deforestation and the caged bird trade. Every minute more rain forest—the habitat of countless birds—is destroyed. The harvesting combines used in toxicant/intensive agriculture leave no food for birds that depend on grains and insects. Every grain is picked up, all insects killed. The birds cannot find food, and they may be poisoned by pesticides and herbicides. Immense numbers of ducks, geese, pheasants and other game birds are shot by hunters. Birds lose food sources to commercial fishing. Oil spills and pollution decimate large numbers of seabirds.

Migratory birds—ducks and geese, herons and egrets, cranes and swans, red knots and terns, puffins and more—

lose stopover places to refuel and rest as we destroy salt marshes, tidal flats and other coastal environments for development. Climate change causes plants to bloom earlier. Migratory birds are out-of-phase with the growing season, and they cannot feed their young. Heat waves, droughts, forest fires and flooding, all more frequent and severe with climate change, bring death to birds everywhere. Ocean acidification destroys food sources for seabirds.

The fate of migratory land animals reveals the devastating impact of climate change, human population growth and lifestyle choices on Nature. The northern caribou starve; freezing rain has replaced snow, and it forms ice over the lichen that they eat. The wildebeest, zebras and gazelles that depend on the Mara River for water during their annual migration may not survive. The watershed of the Mara River, the Mau Forest in Kenya, is being destroyed by people, and this could cause the Mara to disappear. In the western United States, fenced grazing land and highways interrupt the migration route of pronghorns.

Climate change brings hunger/starvation/death to wildlife. Ringed seals, an important food source for polar bears, breed on the ice and make dens there. The melting ice forces the young seals to leave their dens too soon; the polar bears go hungry. Baleen whales, many fish species, crab eater seals, otters, walruses, and some dolphin and porpoise species depend on krill. Myriad extinctions could result from the decline in the number of krill.

On land warmer temperatures cause invasive plant species to crowd out native species that were food sources for wildlife. Cheatgrass has spread across the western United States, for example; in addition to replacing native plants, it is tinder for fires.

In 1900 there were 600% more ocean fish than in 2009. Commercial fishing the last 55 years has brought about a 90% decline in populations of the ocean's top predatory fish, including bluefin tuna, swordfish, marlin and king mackerel. Huge factory ships, designed to catch three times more fish than is sustainable, kill immense numbers of fish with gill nets, trammel nets and longline hooks; trawlers destroy the ocean floor.

The concept of sustainable fishing fails to consider human vegetarian physiology, health risks of animal protein consumption, suffering caused by fish hooks, fish unnecessarily caught to feed factory farm pigs and chickens, and by-kill. When prey disappear, predators such as seabirds, cetaceans, polar bears, otters, walruses and seals go hungry, starve. Sea otters and dolphins and porpoises and seabirds die when tangled in commercial fishing nets or caught with fish hooks. Ocean pollution, from toxic waste to trash to noise, kills marine life; thousands of sea otters died after the Exxon Valdez oil spill, for instance.

Hunting causes innumerable deaths and many extinctions. Our ancestors possibly hunted large carnivores like mastodons and saber-toothed tigers to extinction. Populations of the great cats have greatly decreased. As recently as the 1960s, there were 700,000 leopards; only 50,000 remain. In the last 100 years the number of tigers declined from 100,000 to 3,000.

Elephants and walruses are hunted for their tusks, hippopotamuses for their canines and incisors, meat, or simply shot because they eat rice; a high percentage are wounded, left to suffer before dying. Rhinoceroses are killed for their horns. Peccaries and tapirs are being hunted to extinction. Many primates are hunted for bushmeat and for the cage trade, to where they are at risk of extinction. Sharks are killed in huge numbers for their fins.

A billion people depend on wildlife for food. Education is urgently needed to inform people of the health risks of animal protein consumption, the dire circumstances of wildlife, and to teach farmers worldwide organic vegan farming methods.

An animal-based diet destroys untold animals. The domestication of cattle brought about the extinction of wild bovid species and other large ungulates. Countless deaths continue to occur as rain forests are destroyed to clear land to graze cattle—competition with livestock is one of the main reasons for the dramatic decline in wildlife the past four decades. Worldwide, tens of billions of factory farm animals are killed yearly. Toxicant/intensive agriculture kills innumerable animals by poisoning them, destroying food sources and, in runoffs to lakes and the sea, causing eutrophic water which leads to dense plant populations that, in decomposition, deprive animals of oxygen.

Jack, a goat, and Charlie, a horse, lived at an animal rescue sanctuary (*Animal Odd Couples*). When Charlie started going blind, Jack volunteered to be his seeing-eye goat. Without being trained, Jack knew how to guide Charlie, adjusting his position beside Charlie when Charlie went blind in both eyes. For sixteen years, until Charlie's death, Jack was his devoted helper and friend, showing empathy, kindness and intelligence. Jack and Charlie and all animals simply want to live their lives.

There is hope. People are working around the world to help animals. The number of conservation and animal welfare organizations is heartening, and farm animal groups work ceaselessly to stop the abuse on factory farms. In early October, 2016, CITES (Convention on International Trade in Endangered Species) stopped the legal sale of stockpiled elephant tusks and banned trade in endangered African grey parrots and pangolins. Endangered thresher sharks and several species of manta rays can no longer be fished unless the fishing is proven to be sustainable.

China has banned ivory trade, though illegal smuggling continues. Conservation groups are using drones to track poachers. Botswana and other African nations are seeking a complete ban on ivory trade. Airlines responded to Cecil the Lion's killing by refusing to ship animal trophies. There are concerted efforts to reforest the tropical forests, and sanctuaries have been established for orphaned orangutans, elephants, and more. Tigers are rebounding to a degree thanks to conservation efforts. The Ringling Brothers Circus has stopped using elephants. There is a vaccine to control wildlife populations, and a procedure to sterilize young male dogs.

# REVERENCE FOR LIFE

Our most remarkable quality is our capacity to love. When that love extends beyond ourselves to all animals, all life, the seemingly impossible becomes possible. Our spectacular brains, at the service of compassion, kindness and generosity, can effect wonders.

It is time to weed out selfishness, arrogance and cruelty from our hearts and minds, time for kindness and compassion to guide every action we take as individuals and as a society. Reverence for life makes miracles happen. Reverence for life is the gateway to change, igniting in our hearts the desire and determination to do everything possible to save life on Earth. Reverence for life kindles a hope that energizes action and the belief that one can—must —make a difference, a belief that illuminates one way then another to help save the animals.

*To Save the Animals*

# *SOURCES*

## BOOKS

Attenborough, David. *Life in the Undergrowth.* Princeton: Princeton University Press, 2005.

Attenborough, David. *The Private Life of Plants.* Princeton: Prince University Press, 1995.

Baur, Gene. *Farm Sanctuary: Changing Hearts and Minds about Animals.* New York: Simon and Schuster/Touchstone Books, 2008.

Bortolottis, Dan. *Wild Blue: A Natural History of the World's Largest Animal.* New York: St. Martin's Press, 2008.

Bradley, Fern Marshall, Barbara W. Ellis and Ellen Phillips, editors. *Rodale's Ultimate Encyclopedia of Organic Gardening.* New York: Rodale, Inc., 2009.

Britton, Sarah. *My New Roots: Inspired Plant-based Recipes for Every Season.* New York: Clarkson Potter/Publishers, 2015.

Brown, Jenny, with Gretchen Primack. *The Lucky Ones.* New York: Penguin Group, 2013.

Campbell, T. Colin, PhD, and Thomas M. Campbell II. *The China Study: Startling Implications for Diet, Weight Loss and Long-Term Health.* Dallas: BenBella Books, Inc., 2006.

Campbell, T. Colin, PhD, with Howard Jacobson, PhD. *Whole: Rethinking the Science of Nutrition.* Dallas: BenBella Books, Inc., 2013.

Chamovitz, Daniel. *What a Plant Knows: A Field Guide to the Senses.* New York: Scientific American/ Farrar, Strauss & Giroux, 2012.

Cox, Brian and Andrew Cohen. *Wonders of the Universe.* New York: Harper Collins Publishers, 2011.

Dawkins, Richard. *The Ancestor's Tale: A Pilgrimage to the Dawn of Evolution.* New York: Houghton Mifflin Company, 2004.

Frances, Peter, Senior Editor and Jill Hamilton, U.S. Senior Editor. *Bird: The Definitive Visual Guide* (Audubon). New York: DK Publishing, 2007.

Frances, Peter and Angeles Gavira Guerrero, Senior Editors. *Ocean: the World's Last Wilderness Revealed,* Introduction by Fabien Cousteau (American Museum of Natural History). New York: DK Publishing, 2006.

Goodall, Jane, and Marc Bekoff. *The Ten Trusts: What We Must Do to Care for the Animals We Love.* San Francisco: Harper, 2002.

Goodall, Jane, with Phillip Berman. *Reason for Hope - a Spiritual Journey.* New York: Warner Books, 1999.

Gray, Theodore. *The Elements: A Visual Exploration of Every Known Atom in the Universe.* New York: Black Dog and Leventhal Publishers, 2009.

Grimsrud, Eric P. *Thoughts of a Scientist, Citizen, and Grandpa on Climate Change: Bridging the Gap between Scientific and Public Opinion.* New York and Bloomington: iUniverse, Inc., 2009.

Halliday, Tim and Kraig Adler, editors. *Reptiles and Amphibians.* London: Firefly Books Ltd., 2002.

Hanh, Thich Nhat. *You Are Here: Discovering the Magic of the Present Moment.* Boston and London: Shambhala Publications, Inc., 2011.

Klein, Donna. *The Mediterranean Vegan Kitchen.* New York: The Penguin Group, 2001.

Kolbert, Elizabeth. *The Sixth Extinction: An Unnatural History.* New York: Picador, 2014.

Kostyal, K.M. *Great Migrations: Official Companion to the National Geographic Channel Global Television Event.* Washington, D.C.: National Geographic, 2010.

Lovelock, James. *The Vanishing Face of Gaia.* New York: Basic Books, 2009.

Macdonald, David W., editor. *The Princeton Encyclopedia of Mammals.* Princeton: Princeton University Press, 2006 (paperback 2009, 2013).

Morell, Virginia. *Animal Wise: The Thoughts and Emotions of our Fellow Creatures.* New York: Crown Publishers,2013.

Moskowitz, Isa Chandra and Terry Hope Romero. *Veganomicon: The Ultimate Vegan Cookbook.* Cambridge, MA: Da Capo Press, 2007.

Pacelle, Wayne. *The Humane Economy: How Innovators and Enlightened Consumers Are Transforming the Lives of Animals*. New York: William Morrow, Harper Collins Publishers, 2016.

Parker, Steve. *The Human Body Book*. New York: DK Publishing (American edition), 2007.

Pepperberg, Irene M. *Alex and Me*. New York: Harper-Collins Publishers, 2008.

Perrins, Christopher, editor. *The Princeton Encyclopedia of Birds*. Princeton: Princeton University Press, 2004.

Peterson, Dale. *The Moral Lives of Animals*. New York: Bloomsbury Press, 2011.

Prothero, Donald R. *After the Dinosaurs: The Age of Mammals*. Bloomington: Indiana University Press, 2006.

Redmond, Ian. *The Primate Family Tree*. London: Firefly Books Ltd, Marshall Edition, 2008.

Weston, Chris. *Animals on the Edge: Reporting from the Frontline of Extinction*. New York: Thames and Hudson, 2009.

Wolpert, Lewis. *How We Live & Why We Die: The Secret Lives of Cells*. New York: W. W. Norton & Company, Inc., 2009 (American Edition) .

# DOCUMENTARIES

*www.acidtestmovie.com*. *Natural Resources Defense Council.*

*Animal Childhood* (2015). PBS: Nature Series.

*Animal Odd Couples (*2013*).* PBS: Nature Series.

*[The] Blue Planet: Seas of Life* (2007), narrated by David Attenborough. A BBC/Discovery Channel Co-Production.

*Cowspiracy* (2015), directed by Kip Anderson and Keegan Kuhn. A.U.M. Films

*Death on a Factory Farm: Animal Rights on Trial* (2009), by Tom Simon and Sarah Teale. Home Box Office, Inc.

*[A] Delicate Balance: The Truth* (2008), written and directed by Aaron Scheibner.

*Forks Over Knives (*2011*),* by Lee Fulkerson. Monica Beach Media. (can be watched for free at *www.forksoverknives.com*).

*Great Migrations (*2010), narrated by Peter Coyote. National Geographic Television and Film.

*Island of Lemurs: Madagascar* (2015), narrated by Morgan Freeman. Imax.

*Jane Goodall's When Animals Talk* (2008). Animal Planet. Discovery Communications, LLC.

*[The] Last Lions* (2011), written and directed by Dereck Joubert. Virgin Films and Entertainment, LLC.

*[The] Last Orangutan Eden* (2015), written and produced by Joseph Pontecorvo. THIRTEEN Productions, LLC.

*Life* (2010), narrated by David Attenborough, 4 discs. British Broadcasting Corporation.

*Life in Cold Blood* (2008), narrated by David Attenborough, 2 discs. BBC.

*Life in the Undergrowth* (2005), narrated by David Attenborough, 2 discs. BBC.

*Lizard Kings* (2009). PBS: Nova Series.

*Love in the Animal Kingdom* (2013). PBS: Nature Series.

*Magic of the Snowy Owl* (2012), by Chris Morgan. PBS: Nature Series.

*Mass Extinction: Life at the Brink* (2014), written, directed, edited, produced by Sarah Holt. Tangled Bank Studios, in association with Smithsonian Networks and Holt Productions.

*My Life As a Turkey* (2011), by David Allen. PBS Nature Series.

*Mystery Monkeys of Shangri-La* (2015). PBS: Nature Series.

*Ocean Giants: The Fascinating Lives of Whales and Dolphins* (2011). BBC.

*[A] River of Waste: The Hazardous Truth About Factory Farms* (2009), directed by Don McCorkell. Cinema Libre Studio.

*[The] Salt of the Earth: A Journey with Sebastian Salgado* (2014), by Wim Wenders and Juliano Ribeiro Salgado. Decia Films and Amazonas Images.

*Saving Otter 501* (2013) by Josh Rosen. PBS: Nature Series.

*Sperm Whale* (2012). PBS: Inside Nature's Giants Series. Windfall Films, Ltd.

*Super Cat, Game of Lions, Battle for the Elephants, The Rhino War,Africa: Wilds of Madagascar* (2012-2013). National Geographic, NGC Networks, LLC.

*Unlikely Animal Friends,* 2 discs (2009, 2011, 2012). NGC Networks US, LLC.

*[The] Unlikely Leopard* (2012), narrated by Jeremy Irons. NGHT, LLC.

*Wild Brazil: Land of Fire and Flood* (2014), narrated by Stephen Mangan. BBC Earth, a BBC/Discovery Channel co-production.

*Wild Congo* (2014). National Geo Wild, NGC Networks US, LLC.

*Years of Living Dangerously* (2014). TV Series by James Cameron, Jerry Weintraub and Arnold Schwartzenegger, originally aired on Showtime.

# ARTICLES

Baraniuk, Chris. "How Do We Know That Evolution Is Really Happening?". *BBC Earth*, August 11, 2015, retrieved August 12, 2015, 3:23 p.m.

Briggs, Helen, BBC environment correspondent. "Wildlife decline may lead to 'empty landscape'". *BBC News/Science and Environment*. May 2, 2015, retrieved October 28, 2015, 5:31 p.m.

"Earth has lost half of its wildlife in the past 40 years, says WWF". *The Guardian*, September 30, 2014, retrieved October 28, 2015, 5:38 p.m.

Foer, Joshua. "Thinking Like a Dolphin: Understanding One of the Smartest Creatures on Earth". *National Geographic*, May 2015, 30-55.

Genoways, Ted. "Gagged by Big Ag". *Mother Jones*, July/August 2013.

Germanos, Andrea, staff writer. "Report: Climate *Change* Has Already Brought Catastrophe to US Wildlife". Common Dreams, January 30, 2013, email.

Germanos, Andrea, staff writer. "The Solution to Climate Change Right Under Our Feet". *Common Dreams*, April 27, 2015, email.

Gill, Victoria. "Are These Animals Too "Ugly" to Be Saved?" *BBC/Science and Environment*, November 20, 2012, retrieved November 23, 2012, 4:12 p.m.

Goodland, Robert and Jeff Anhang. "Livestock and Climate Change". *World Watch,* November/December 2009. www.worldwatch.org.

Heikkinen, Nina. "Ocean's Oxygen Starts Running Low". *Scientific American*/Climate Wire, 5.2.2016, retrieved 5.10.16, 7:03 p.m.

Harrabin, Roger, BBC environment analyst. "World Wildlife Populations Halved in 40 Years". *BBC/Science and Environment*, September 30, 2014, retrieved October 28, 5:30 p.m.

Lovejoy, Thomas E. "The Climate Change Endgame". *The New York Times*, January 21, 2013.

Mooney, Chris. 'The most singular thing we have found': Clouds study alarms scientists. *The Washington Post*, 7.15.16, retrieved 7.15.16, 9:49 a.m.

Mooney, Chris. "This new Antarctica study is bad news for climate change doubters". *Washington Post*, 7.5.16, retrieved 7.7.16, 9:08 a.m.

"One Third of Fish Caught Worldwide Used As Animal Feed". *The Telegraph,* October 29, 2008, retrieved December 8, 2015, 10:35 a.m.

Pollan, Michael. "The Intelligent Plant: Scientists Debate a New Way of Understanding Flora". *The New Yorker*, December 23, 2013.

Safina, Carl. "Big Love". *Orion*, May/June 2015, 42-51.

Solie, Stacey. "Scientists Adopt Tiny Island as a
  Warming Bellwether". *The New York Times*,
  October 6, 2012.

Steinfeld, Henning et al. *Livestock's Long Shadow:
  Environmental Issues and Options*. Livestock,
  Environment and Development (LEAD) Initiative, Food
  and Agriculture Organization of the United Nations.
  Rome, 2006.

Stuart, A., A.C. Short, D. Inkley, I. Ricker. *Wildlife in
  a Warming World: Confronting the Climate Crisis*.
  Washington, D.C.: National Wildlife Federation, 2013.

*Technical Report for 3rd National Climate Assessment*.
  "Impacts of Climate Change on *Biodiversity, Ecosystems,
  and Ecosystem* Services", posted by Jordan Carlton Schaul
  of *Wildlife SOS*, January 10, 2013.

"Texas and Kansas Farmers Take Different Paths to
  Saving Waste". *Circle of Blue News*, retrieved
  December 13, 2015, 4:00 p.m.

"The 15 Tweaks That Made Us Human". *BBC Earth*,
  March 14, 2015, retrieved March 15, 2015, 1:05 p.m.

"Too much protein could lead to early death, study
  says". *The Washington Post*, March 4, 2014,
  retrieved September 16, 2015, 1:45 p.m.

Unferth, Deb Olin. "Cage Wars: A Visit to the Egg Farm".
  *Harper's*, November 2014, 43-52.

"Use It and Lose It: The Outsize Effect of US Consumption on the Environment". *Scientific American,* September 14, 2012, retrieved September 26, 2015, 1:22 p.m.

"We've wiped out half the world's wildlife since 1970". *Vox,* updated by Brad Plumer July 29, 2015, 2:10 p.m. ET, retrieved October 28, 2015, 5:37 p.m.

*WWF Living Planet Report 2014* (wwf.panda.org/about_our_earth/all_publications/living_planet_)

Zimmer, Carl. "Secrets of the Brain". *National Geographic,* February 2014, 34-57.

Yulsman, Tom: "Climate in Crisis". *Discover,* January/February 2015, 11-12.

Wikipedia:

*Adenine.* Retrieved January 31, 2015, 4:27 p.m.
*Agriculture.* Retrieved April 4, 2015, 4:18 p.m.
*Amphibian.* Retrieved June 4, 2015, 10:53 a.m.
*Arctic sea ice decline.* Retrieved January 31, 2015, 4:03 p.m.
*Atmosphere.* Retrieved September 17, 2015, 10:23 a.m.
*Atmospheric methane.* Retrieved November 11, 2015, 3:16 p.m.
*Big Bang.* Retrieved September 17, 2015, 10:25 a.m.
*Carbon.* Retrieved July 30, 2015, 9:31 a.m.
*Carnivore.* Retrieved September 25, 2015, 8:16 a.m.
*Cetacea.* Retrieved September 25, 2015, 8:15 a.m.
*Chondrichthyes.* Retrieved September 25, 2015, 8:12 a.m.
*Climate change.* Retrieved March 14, 2015, 3:47 p.m.
*Climate change and agriculture.* Retrieved September 5, 2015, 2:32 p.m.

*Cnidaria.* Retrieved September 25, 2015, 8:11 a.m.
*Cytosine.* Retrieved January 31, 2015, 4:15 p.m.
*Dairy.* Retrieved September 17, 2015, 11:01 a.m.
*Deforestation and Climate Change.* Retrieved
  September 5, 2015, 2:36 p.m.
*Desalination.* Retrieved September 17, 2015, 11:15 a.m.
*Desertification.* Retrieved September 5, 2015, 2:39 p.m.
*DNA.* Retrieved February 5, 2015, 4:57 p.m.
*DNA replication.* Retrieved September 25, 2015, 8:08 a.m.
*Echinoderm.* Retrieved September 24, 2015, 8:11 a.m.
*Elephant.* Retrieved September 5, 2015, 2:42 p.m.
*Embryogenesis.* Retrieved September 25, 2015, 8:08 a.m.
*Endangered species.* Retrieved September 25, 2015,
  8:17 a.m.
*Eukaryote.* Retrieved January 31, 2015, 4:31 p.m.
*Evolutionary history of life.* Retrieved April 23, 2013,
  10:34 a.m.
*Frog.* Retrieved June 4, 2015, 10:52 a.m.
*Gastrulation.* Retrieved September 17, 2015, 11:17 a.m.
*Giraffe.* Retrieved September 25, 2015, 8:22 a.m.
*Global warming.* Retrieved September 5, 2015, 2:47 p.m.
*Greenhouse gas.* Retrieved September 5, 2015, 2:53 p.m.
*Guanine.* Retrieved January 31, 2015, 4:28 p.m.
*Holocene extinction.* Retrieved March 14, 2015, 3:44 p.m.
*Intensive animal farming.* Retrieved September 17, 2015,
  11:32 a.m.
*Invertebrate.* Retrieved September 25, 2015, 8:10 a.m.
*Killing of Cecil the Lion.* Retrieved August 27, 2015,
  11:07 a.m.
*Mammal.* Retrieved September 25, 2015, 8:13 a.m.
*Mangrove.* Retrieved September 25, 2015, 8:18 a.m.
*Meiosis.* Retrieved September 25, 2015, 8:06 a.m.
*Methane.* Retrieved January 7, 2015, 4:02 p.m.
*Mitochondrion.* Retrieved January 31, 2015, 4:29 p.m.
*Mitosis.* Retrieved September 25, 2015, 8:07 a.m.

*Neocortex*. Retrieved September 25, 2015,  8:16 a.m.

*Nitrogen*. Retrieved July 30, 2015, 9:31 a.m.

*Nitrous oxide*. Retrieved January 7, 2015, 4:05 p.m.

*Nutrient pollution*. Retrieved April 27, 2015, 3:38 p.m.

*Ocean acidification.*Retrieved September 17, 2015, 1:42 a.m.

*Organic horticulture.* Retrieved September 25, 2015, 8:15 a.m.

*Osteichthyes*. Retrieved September 24, 2015,  8:13 a.m.

*Pinniped*. Retrieved September 25, 2015, 8:14 a.m.

*Population growth*. Retrieved September 17, 2015, 11:39 a.m.

*Protein*. Retrieved February 15, 2015, 4:58 p.m.

*Seal hunting*. Retrieved August 27, 2015, 11:21 a.m.

*Thymine*. Retrieved January 31, 2015, 4:27 p.m.

*Timeline of plant evolution*. Retrieved August 18, 2014, 10:05 a.m.

*Universe*. Retrieved September 17, 2015, 11:31 a.m.

*Western Antarctic ice sheet*. Retrieved September 17, 2015, 11:39 a.m.

*Wildlife Services*. Retrieved September 26, 2015, 1:07 p.m.

# WEBSITES

## CLIMATE CHANGE/CONSERVATION/ ENVIRONMENT

*www.350.org* - focuses on the need to decrease carbon dioxide.

*www.arkive.org* - films, photos and audio recordings of threatened species, including many profiles.

*www.cites.org* - The Convention on International

Trade in Endangered Species of Wild Fauna
and Flora (CITES), intended to control trade in
wildlife, especially to prevent animals from
becoming threatened with extinction by trade.

*www.citizensclimatelobby.org* - Citizens Climate Lobby

*www.climatecrisiscoalition.org* - Climate Crisis Coalition

*www.climate-justice-now.org* - Climate Justice
  Now!, a global coalition of networks and
  organizations campaigning for climate justice.

*www.climaterealityproject.org* - The Climate Reality Project

*www.conservation.org* - Conservation International,
  describes climate change problems with videos.

*www.dancingstarfoundation.org* - Dancing Star Foundation,
  a U.S.-based non-profit organization engaged in
  environmental, cultural and animal welfare activities.

*www.earthisland.org* - Earth Island Institute, organizes and
  encourages activism around environmental issues and
  provides public education.

*www.earthjustice.org* - Earthjustice, free legal representation
  to citizen groups to enforce environmental laws
  in the United States.

*www.earthwatch.org* - Earthwatch, a non-profit
  environmental organization focused on
  connecting everyday people with the world's
  top scientists to conduct vital field research.

www.edf.org - Environmental Defense Fund, links
  science, economics and law to create
  innovative, equitable and cost-effective
  solutions to the most urgent environment problems.

*www.fauna-flora.org* - Fauna and Flora International,
  supports international conservation activities.

*www.foe.org* - Friends of the Earth, international network
  of environmental organizations

*www.footprintnetwork.org* - Global Footprint Network

*www.fundwildnature.org* - Fund for Wild Nature,
  provides funds to small groups who get things done.

*www.globalwitness.org* - Global Witness

*www.inforse.org* - International Network for
  Sustainable Energy (INFORSE)

*www.ipcc.ch* - Intergovernmental Panel on Climate Change

*www.iucn.org* - International Union for
  Conservation of Nature (IUCN)

*www.iucnredlist.org* - International Union for the
  Conservation of Nature and Natural Resources
  (IUCN) Red List of Threatened and Endangered Species
  website.

*www.letsdoitworld.org* - Let's Do It! World, civic-led
  mass movement to clean up the whole world from illegally
  dumped solid waste and then to keep it clean.

*www.natureserve.org* - NatureServe, provides scientific basis
  for effective conservation action, winner of a
  MacArthur Foundation Award.

*www.npca.org* - National Parks Conservation Association

*www.npg.org* - Negative Population Growth

*www.oceanconservancy.org* - Ocean Conservancy,
  educates and empowers citizens to take action
  on behalf of the ocean.

*www.onegreenplanet.org*

*www.peer.org* - Public Employees for
  Environmental Responsibility (PEER), national
  non-profit alliance of local, state and federal
  scientists, law enforcement officers, land
  managers and other professionals dedicated to
  upholding environmental laws and values.

*www.populationconnection.org* - Population Connection,
  America's voice for population stabilization.

*www.rainforest-alliance.org* - Rainforest Alliance
  International,non- profit organization
  dedicated to the preservation of tropical forests.

*www.rainforesttrust.org* - Rainforest Trust,
  works to protect tropical rain forests.

*www.rootsandshoots.org* - Roots and Shoots

*www.seashepherd.org* - Sea Shepherd
   Conservation Society (SSCS), an international
   non-profit marine wildlife conservation
   organization.

*www.sierraclub.org* - Sierra Club, environmental
   and factory farm issues.

*www.unep.org* - United Nations Environment
   Programme (UNEP)

*www.uscusa.org* - Union of Concerned Scientists

*www.wcs.org* - Wildlife Conservation Society (WCS),
   U.S. organization managing national and international
   conservation projects, research and education programs.

*www.wetlands.org* - Wetlands International, works
   to sustain and restore wetlands, their resources
   and biodiversity.

*www.wilderness.org* - The Wilderness Society,
   dedicated to preserving America's wilderness
   through action and public education.

*www.wno.org* - World Nature Organization
   (WNO), dedicated to the protection of the
   environment at the international level, with
   focus on energy efficiency, climate protection,
   sustainable development and sustainable energy.

*www.worldlandtrust.org* - World Land Trust (WLT),
   international conservation charity that protects
   the world's most biologically and threatened habitats acre
   by acre

*www.worldwatch.org* - Worldwatch Institute,
  works towards sustainability, environmentally sound jobs
  and development, and an end to human population
  growth.

*www.worldwildlife.org* - World Wide Fund for Nature
  (WWF), also known as World Wildlife Fund,
  an international non-governmental organization
  working on conservation, research and environmental
  restoration.

## ANIMALS

*www.aldf.org* - Animal Legal Defense Fund

*www.animalequality.net* - Animal Equality

*www.animalsvoice.com* - Animals' Voice

*www.aspca.org* - American Society for the
  Prevention of Cruelty to Animals (ASPCA)

*www.audubon.org* - National Audubon Society

*www.bestfriends.org* - Best Friends, large no-kill sanctuary.

*www.birdlife.org* - BirdLife International, global
  partnership of conservation organizations that
  aims to conserve birds, bird habitats and global
  biodiversity.

*www.bird-rescue.org* -International Bird Rescue,
  research dedicated to mitigating the human impact
  on aquatic birds and other wildlife worldwide
  through emergency response, education, research
  and planning.

*www.defenders.org* - Defenders of Wildlife

*www.elephantconservation.org* - International
  Elephant Foundation

*www.friendsofanimals.org* - Friends of Animals (FoA)

*www.harpseals.org* - Harp Seals, fighting to end
  the harp seal slaughter.

*www.humanesociety.org* - Humane Society of
  the United States (HSUS), animal protection organization.

*www.idausa.org* - In Defense of Animals (IDA),
  international non-profit dedicated to ending
  institutionalized exploitation and abuse of animals
  by defending their rights, welfare and habitat.

*www.ippl.org* - International Primate Protection League

*www.janegoodall.org* - Jane Goodall Institute

*www.lionalert.org* - Africa Needs Lions

*www.nwf.org* - National Wildlife Federation,
  dedicated to protecting wildlife, habitats and to inspiring
  future generations of conservationists.

*www.mercyforanimals.org* - Mercy for Animals, a non-profit animals advocacy organization dedicated to ending the  exploitation and abuse of animals.

*www.orangutan.org* - Orangutan Foundation International

*www.ourplanettheirstoo.org* - Our Planet Theirs Too (OPTT), a non-profit animal rights and planet conservation organization that presents a new vision of Planet Earth and all of the beings who live on Earth.

*www.peta.org* - People for the Ethical Treatment  of Animals

*www.saveelephant.org* - Save Elephant Foundation

*www.saveelephants.org* - Save the Elephants

*www.96elephants.org* - 96 Elephants, action to save the elephants.

*www.saveourmonarchs.org* - Save Our Monarchs, focused on restoring milkweed one plant at a time.

*www.savethefrogs.com* - Save the Frogs!, world's leading amphibian conservation organization.

*www.savethemanatee.org* - Save the Manatee Club

*www.savetheorangutan.org* - Save the Orangutan

*www.savethewhales.org* - Save the Whales

*www.savetigersnow.org.* - Save Tigers Now, campaign by World Wildlife Fund and Leonardo DiCaprio.

*www.wolf.org* - International Wolf Center

# FARM ANIMALS

*www.ciwf.com* - Compassion in World Farming, international farm animal welfare organization.

*www.cok.net* - Compassion Over Killing, focuses on stopping cruelty to factory farm animals.

*www.cowspiracy.com*

*www.farmedanimal.net* - Farmed Animal Net

*www.farmsanctuary.org* - Farm Sanctuary
*www.farmusa.org* - Farm Animal Rights Movement (FARM), promotes planetary survival through plant-based eating.

*www.hfa.org* - Humane Farming Association (HFA), farm animal protection, information on factory farm abuses, and the nation's largest farm animal refuge.

*www.mercyforanimals.org* - Mercy for Animals, a non-profit animal advocacy organization dedicated to ending the exploitation and abuse of animals.

*www.upc-online.org* - United Poultry Concerns (UPC), activist group that campaigns against cruelty to chickens and other domestic fowl.

# VEGAN

*www.americanvegan.org* - American Vegan Society

*www.animalsvoice.com* - Animals' Voice,
  networking source for animal rights news, etc.

*www.earthsave.org* - EarthSave, promotes food choices
  that are healthy for people and the planet, and helps
  people transition toward a healthy plant-based diet.

*www.farmusa.org* - Farm Animal Rights Movement
  (FARM), promotes planetary survival through plant-
  based eating.

*www.forksoverknives.com* - Forks Over Knives
  film, recipes, information about the health benefits
  of a plant-based diet, and more.

*www.generationveggie.org* - Generation Veggie,
  guidance on raising children with a  plant-based diet.

*www.onegreenplanet.org*

*www.pcrm.org* - Physicians Committee for
  Responsible Medicine

*www.peta.org* - People for the Ethical Treatment
  of Animals

*www.plantbased.org* - Institute for Plant-Based Nutrition

*www.veganorganic.net* - Vegan Organic Network,
  information on vegan organic farming, vegetable compost,
  green manures, crop rotation, mulches, etc.

*www.veganoutreach.org* - Vegan Outreach

*www.vegansociety.com* - Vegan Society

*To Save the Animals*